NON-FICTION FOR NEWBIES

HOW TO WRITE A FACTUAL BOOK AND ACTUALLY KIND OF ENJOY IT

LAUREN BINGHAM

CONTENTS

INTRODUCTION

"But basically, you just tell everybody whatever happened. What was said. What was done. It's all right there. You don't need to make anything up. It's got to be way easier than writing a story where you have to make up a magical land and draw maps and invent languages and whatever."

My friend was trying to understand why I was frazzled after doing a final editing push with a 30,000-word nonfiction piece. I'm not even sure "frazzled" is the best word to use. I love my job, but there's this adrenaline rush that comes at the end of a book, then the tension of the editing tap dance, and once it's all said and done, you choose the cover for your book and fall into a sort of fugue state or stupor.

It was this state of mind that inspired my response of "Whaa...? No, but you... it doesn't just happen. You have to write it."

My friend nodded sympathetically. "There, there," he said, reaching across the cafe table to pat my hand lovingly. "Let's just get you a yummy dessert with some chocolate in it."

The healing properties of chocolate did, in fact, revive me, and I was able to explain some of the challenges of writing nonfiction in actual words and concepts. Eventually, I was able to convince him that the rumors were not true: writing nonfiction is just as hard, and in some ways even harder, than writing fiction pieces.

Nonfiction indeed comes from a place of reality. It may be spun, twisted, distorted, edited, or even censored, but somewhere in there is a real person, place, or situation. The reader is drawn to these books because they want to read about something very specific and very real that has touched them in some way. For example, you're likely reading this book because you are interested in the process behind writing nonfiction books.

Writing about reality is an art form. Let's take a look at the start of this book, and my retelling of my encounter with a friend. That really happened. We could consider this as part of a longer autobiographical piece or memoir, depending on the journey I took with it. It's nonfiction.

I "told everybody what happened" in the most pedantic sense of the phrase. In a "too long; didn't read (tl;dr)" world, my story is quite simple: my friend and I met at a cafe after I hit a big career milestone, and he attempted to console me by telling me my job wasn't as hard as others in my profession. Also, there was chocolate.

Both my version and the tl;dr version are valid works of nonfiction. They convey the point. The difference is that one sets the scene in detail, outlining my psychological state, the warm intentions of my friend, and the myth that I quickly squelched. The other is the pamphlet version of the scene--a brief vignette that highlights the most necessary details.

Neither way is right nor wrong. However, as a fledgling nonfiction writer, you will need to decide how you're going to write your piece. Are you going to maintain that brevity is the soul of wit, or are you the type to paint a detailed picture with your words? You may also be somewhere in between—carefully choosing to elaborate here while trimming back the detail there to advance the discussion.

Those who have read my earlier books on the topic of writing- *How to Write a Book: A Book for Anyone Who Has Never Written a Book (But Wants To)* or *One Word at a Time: How to Write a Fiction Book for Beginners*- will appreciate that my definition of "how to" is a little different than others–another reflection of a decision you will have to make if you choose this path. I'm not able to hold your hand as you type to make sure that you put the perfect word in the perfect place every time. If I had that skill, this book would cost a great deal more. Instead, I'm going to coax you through the challenges, pump you up for progress, and agonize with you when it seems like nothing is calling you to be written. I will be honest and candid about the process and suggest strategies to help you get through the difficult parts.

We won't be going through topics like fact-checking, choosing the best adverb, or nonfiction-style theories. Instead, we'll look at the major types of nonfiction, including:

- Biographies, Autobiographies, Memoirs

- History and Travel

- Self-Help and How-To

- Philosophy, and Insight/Analysis

We'll look at what each of these types of work entails, as well as the various decisions writers may encounter when working on one of these pieces. The decisions you make as you write are always your own, and I encourage you to write exactly what you need to write. You can always go back and edit your work. Today's computing technology even allows us to save version histories so we don't lose any of our changes along the way. You can change your mind any time you want, so write from the heart and worry about it all working out later!

That being said, you can pull the final product together better if you are prepared for the questions and challenges you'll face along the way. A successful nonfiction piece is one that fulfills the dream of the author. It makes the right points, shares distinct information, asks the reader to consider the topic in greater detail, and can even challenge the reader's view of reality. Nonfiction work can be powerful, which is why I recommend that if you intend to write your own nonfiction piece, you aim to write a good one, whatever your personal definition of "good" may be. I do have a few ideas I would like to share with you on that topic.

In order to outfit you with the right tools for your writing journey, we'll take a look at some of the ways you can set yourself up for feeling good about your first nonfiction effort, from putting together your outline and choosing your style to gain helpful hints based on the various nonfiction genres.

I encourage all writers to read all chapters. You may be dead set on becoming a biographer, and I wish you all the best in that endeavor. But there's a chance that some of the thoughts I share in the "how-to" chapter may help you make decisions about your own piece. My own writing mentor encouraged me to not only read things that I wanted to read but to also read things I'd never considered. By doing so, I would be able to appreciate a greater range of styles, voices, tones, and approaches to different topics. He was absolutely correct—nearly every piece I write is partially inspired by something I've only just discovered in the process of writing that very book. From a turn of phrase to the pacing of the words, each book I write is a collection of everything I've learned since the previous effort.

My goal is to help you feel as confident in yourself as you can as a person who is starting to write a piece of nonfiction. As I've noted in my previous books, writing is a highly emotional, cerebral, and physical process. While I can't make the process any easier, I can be your writing buddy who can give you a tour through every step. I'll give you all the spoilers and do everything I can to ease your anxiety about the process.

Whether or not you write the next best seller after reading this book depends on a lot of factors. But I hope you feel inspired to start working on the outline for your nonfiction piece. And then, I hope you decide to keep going and research your topic and then start fleshing out the chapters. Write it. Stop worrying about it, and write it. But first, let's get acquainted with the task at hand.

What Makes "Good" Nonfiction?

I am oddly sensitive about the word "good." I know this isn't a book about what I, personally, like and don't like, but the word "good" is bandied about frequently in everyday conversation.

When referring to their first book, most first-time authors express the hope that it's "good," or "decent," or that it "doesn't suck." These are excellent aspirations in theory, but they don't really mean anything in the grand scheme of things.

Terms like "good" or "decent" and a book's suckitude—or lack thereof—are all vague and subjective. What is "good?" The opposite of "bad?" Ok, so what's "bad?" And then we tumble into a weird psycho-philosophical debate about conditional measurement and lived experiences. It gets messy fast.

When folks say they want to write a book that is good/decent/doesn't suck, they generally mean that they want to write a book that people want to read. People generally want to read books that they enjoy reading, page by page. That is, they want to enjoy the entire process, not slug through a few thousand words until they get to the good stuff.

This means that things like pace, tone, and style matter. The words you use are important. The way words flow, the conventions that you describe or omit, your grasp of grammar, and your ability to tell a story are still very important, even if the story you're telling is 100% factual.

"Pace" refers not only to the timeline of your book but to how quickly or slowly the average reader will be able to digest the content. Let's say, for example, you're writing a biography and wish to cover events from your subject's entire lifetime. You're going to have to consider how much time to devote to each section of your subject's life and which events to delve deeper into while skimming over others.

The tone of your book may be somewhat consistent, or it may shift depending on the topic at hand. You may approach certain topics with levity while providing very serious or shocking revelations about others. The words you choose help to set the tone. Consider, if you will, the difference between Snoopy's favorite "dark and stormy night" and "the sun, cracked in two by the horizon like an egg, spilling out light," as experienced by Margaret Atwood. These phrases represent not just opposite times of day, but two very different tones. It is the writers' artful manipulation of the words that set these unique tones.

"Style" is somewhat of an umbrella term for the process through which you choose the words you choose, put them in a particular order, shuffle them around until you find the version you like best, and keep going until you've run out of things to say. That may seem like a bit of a simultaneously direct and evasive answer, but style is very unique to every creator. The way you decorate your bedroom, the way you dress, how you take your coffee, and how you write are all part of your very own independent style. Your style may be heavily influenced by other individuals, but ultimately, what appears on the screen or paper in front of you is entirely your own.

There are ways to develop your pace, tone, and style, which I've discussed in my other books. If you've had a chance to read those, some of this information may seem familiar. The best way to develop anything, however, is to practice! Write away! Don't worry whether it's "good" or even "good enough." Instead, write because you want the practice. Visual artists have sketchbooks, so it stands to reason that those of us who work with words need practice as well. Get yourself a lovely notebook and supportive seat cushion, and write as much and as frequently as you feel called to write. Before you know it, you'll start feeling increasingly comfortable.

For those of us writing nonfiction pieces, pace, tone, and style are incredibly important. We use these devices to keep our readers reading. However, these aren't the only things to keep in mind when getting ready to write your nonfiction debut.

Let's take a deeper look into some of the most crucial factors to consider when planning your new literary venture.

A Shiny Topic

All of us aspire to be the kind of author who can write a book so beautifully that the audience won't care that it's incredibly boring. We want to believe we can take any mundane topic and polish it into incandescence with our carefully honed writing skills.

At the end of the day, however, we need to recognize the reality that current SEO recommendations include paragraphs that are at most three lines of text or two sentences. We've trained our brains to look for keywords, and our shrunken attention span is being pulled in multiple directions simultaneously. Perhaps you can write an absolutely stunning book about paint drying, but if you want to sell it, you've got to be a marketing genius. (You've also got to email me if you try this because I would love to hear your plans.)

Your choice of topic matters for so many reasons. If you choose an incredibly broad topic, you'll find yourself writing in overlapping circles trying to explain everything, creating a labyrinth of thought that will leave your audience trying to piece the details back together. Additionally, a broad topic requires a long time to explain. If you are working on a shorter essay, you may find that cramming a lot of details into a small space means you have to leave some information behind. Similarly, selecting a very specific topic for a longer article or book may force you to repeat yourself and stuff a bunch of unnecessary fluff into your writing just to meet the word count.

Furthermore, what is your angle on the topic? What particular details are you going to focus on in your nonfiction book? If you're writing a biographical piece on a political figure, for example, what aspects of their life are you going to highlight? What details of their political stance will you examine, and by what light? Are you writing from the standpoint of someone who agrees with this figure, or are you critiquing their actions?

Long ago, I took a writing class in which we pulled topics out of a plastic Jack-O-Lantern each month. We would then take our shiny new topics to the library and start to research. The goal was to write a different style of research piece involving that topic, but the topics themselves were astonishingly broad.

I once chose a slip of paper upon which the word "Madonna" had been typed. That's it. I had to choose whether I was going to write about Madonna, Mother of Christ, or Madonna, Queen of Pop. Then, I had to decide where I was going to go from there—there's no shortage of material on either of these remarkable women. I narrowed it down to comparing various historical artistic depictions of the Virgin Mary or detailing Madonna Ciccone's relationship with her mother—who passed away when Madonna was five years old—in the face of her own pregnancy announcement (long ago, remember). I chose the latter because the assignment had a ten-page limit, and I couldn't trust myself not to pick too many art samples.

The topic you select will appeal to a wide range of readers. The focus you choose will reduce the number of interested parties, but those who read it will likely be extremely interested and engaged. The angle you take will determine whether they write you nasty emails later.

Whether you're writing a biography, a history, a travel piece, or a how-to book, there will be some who agree with your observations and some who strongly do not. They won't necessarily write you nasty emails later—that was a bit of hyperbole, since the distribution of your book may be as minimal or global as you wish. However, if your goal is to write a "good" book, you'll need to prepare for some people to not find it that "good," after all.

You might think that writing nonfiction should be pretty neutral territory since you aren't making anything up—these are real people and things that you're writing about, after all! But even your most respectful, thoughtful, fact-driven writing will be bound to evoke some feelings. Many times, these feelings have nothing to do with your actual writing, but the realizations and thoughts that the reader had while they were digesting your piece.

Sometimes we write incendiary pieces on purpose. Persuasive pieces are fun, as are shocking exposes. If you've ever written a negative review for a business, you know the thrill of honestly emoting in the form of critique. Writing is art, and our emotions nearly always come peeking out in our craft. The angle you take when approaching your subject already speaks volumes about your thought process, so do you want to go for it and expose your true feelings, or play it neutral to appeal to a wider audience?

Consider who you want to read this book. Who are you speaking to? Who do you want to understand your message? Who do you think is going to read this book and take away all of the fine points and details you have written? Who is going to emotionally and mentally connect with your writing?

You may find that the angle from which you're approaching your topic and your audience don't really match well. The ten-page essay about Madonna and maternal relations would have been very different depending on who I wrote it for—I ended up choosing a high school audience because many of the interviews I found in my research discussed the pop singer feeling awkward in high school due to not having a mother figure in her life. I wanted to use this approach to connect with the insecurity we all feel during our teenage years, which can be amplified by any sense of being "strange."

Sometimes, writing feels like a puzzle. You've got lots of pieces sitting before you, and you just need to make them all fit. I think of brainstorming a topic more like looking through a kaleidoscope. You can clearly see what you're focused on at the end, but the light and mirrors play tricks on you, and the picture shifts any time you shift positions. As you're choosing your topic, I recommend rotating the lens a bit so you can view it from different angles. Focus on all sorts of different details, then spin the kaleidoscope to see the myriad of ways you can present your specific topic to your specific audience to get the desired effect.

Start conservative—what are some of the obvious topics you could choose? What is the first thing that comes to mind when you think about a specific issue, time period, or event? Some things are inextricably linked for better or worse, such as the Titanic and icebergs or Theodore Roosevelt and the National Park Service. But, of course, there's more to each of those topics than their existence or relationship to each other.

There are many ways to brainstorm your topic. Some writers use something like a Venn diagram, in which they start linking together interests and shifting angles to see how they lead back into each other. Others start with lists, with sub-topics branching off of each other, somewhat like a sports championship bracket. Still, others take advantage of the many technological advances that allow us to stay organized and write without losing track of all of our best ideas, such as writing apps, spreadsheets, and voice recorders. In one remarkable case, I knew a writer who would videotape herself talking through her topic.

If you're not sure where to start with all of these potential techniques, I recommend going back to the roots of writing with the analog paper-and-pencil technique. Find a blank piece of paper and a writing utensil of your choice, and jot down the first thing you think of when you think of writing a book. Abraham Lincoln. How to organize your closet. The way doing yoga daily saved your relationship. The history of Velcro.

Don't think too much about it. Don't worry about whether you should put the words in the middle of the page or at the top left or cattywampus across the entire right side. This isn't about doing things right. It's about doing them at all, and it's now that you are summoning the energy that is going to get you through this new book experience.

Now that you've got that idea down, write down everything that comes to mind after it. This "mind spew" can take the form of entire, cohesive sentences, clips and phrases, single words, or even drawings.

This is going to be harder than you expect because the judgemental pieces of your brain are going to try to talk you out of everything:

- *"You don't think anyone has examined Abraham Lincoln's mental health?"*

- *"Do you honestly believe there are 30,000 words about how flip flops changed the world?"*

- *"You are the only person who would read this."*

- *"You are not qualified to write about this topic."*

This very same voice has silenced some of the greatest authors who have never been published. Ignore it.

In fact, if you have a particularly poignant thought on your topic, go ahead and open a new document on your computer. Call it whatever you want. "New Book" is just fine. I've titled the first draft of this book "Nonfiction MS" because I haven't chosen the final title, and that's likely where you are now. Remove all thoughts of the finished book for now, and start typing out the words that need to be released. As I type this paragraph, I have no idea what the cover of this book will look like or even what it will look like after it goes through a few rounds of editing. There are pages of content you will never read because that's the reality of writing. Your document will live and breathe until it's published, and then it continues to live and breathe in the minds and hearts of its readers.

When the book starts calling, answer. Start typing. Start listing. Start drawing. Keep the conversation going with yourself, but don't pick at yourself if you run out of ideas. That just means you need to approach it from another angle.

Sometimes I don't really know how finely tuned my topic is going to be until I've started outlining the table of contents. There have even been times when I'm actively drafting the introduction and then realized that I needed to adjust a few things in order to make a coherent book appear.

At the same time, it's easy to think too much. If you try to apply too much logic to the art of choosing a topic, you will talk yourself out of the task. Whether I'm writing for myself or a client, my choice of topic, book organization, and research patterns depend on so many different factors—keywords, what's trending, and what I really want to write about. And ultimately, every time I sit down to write a book, it starts with a messy sheet of paper where I built the foundation by excavating the perfect topic.

So what is the "perfect topic?" In my opinion, it's the sweet spot where your passion and your interests collide with an inexplicable need to share this information with the entire world. In many cases, it's entirely illogical, which is why it's so easy to talk yourself out of doing it in the first place.

Writing a nonfiction book of any kind is going to take patience, time, energy, research, and careful planning. If you aren't all that invested in the topic, this will be agonizing. If you're mild to moderately interested in the topic, you might find yourself growing fond of and more fascinated by the topic as you uncover new details each time you dive into research. If you're moderately to severely obsessed with the topic, you'll find yourself trying to hold back before you go into encyclopedia mode. It's not that I don't encourage you to do so—I've just never written an encyclopedia, so I have no special advice for you!

But if you're planning on writing a biography, autobiography, memoir, history, travel, self-help, how-to, philosophy, or insight/analysis book, I've got you covered. Choose a topic that will stick. Start broad with a topic you could discuss in your sleep. Narrow it down. Cogitate on it. Ask yourself questions. Jot down your thoughts. Give it a few days, but not too many. Try typing a few paragraphs about it to try it on for size. If you don't find yourself getting sick of smartphone news alerts bringing up your topic every waking moment while you do this, you might just be onto something very good.

Fresh Perspective

The concept of perspective goes hand-in-hand with your topic. Essentially, the perspective is the angle from which you view your topic, and through which you interpret all data and research to support your topic. Ideally, every writer will have a different perspective, which when combined with their unique voice and particular style allows for us to have many books that cover the same topic without them being word-for-word identical to each other.

There are very few topics that haven't been covered in some manner, which is why I urge you to ignore the voice of logic while you're hashing out your topic. I am completely aware that this is not the one and only "how to write nonfiction" book in the world. There are plenty of resources out there which cover all of the things I'll discuss in the following pages. If you have been researching this topic for a while, then you likely will not be surprised by the content of this book.

That being said, no one is going to write a book like I write a book. At least, I would prefer they didn't. My voice, tone, style, vocabulary, insistence on using "too," "very," and "so" so very too much, and examples are (hopefully) different from the experience you've had reading any other book on the matter.

Books inform and entertain, though each book offers a different ratio of each. For example, your seventh-grade history textbook was primarily written to inform, though the occasional witty quote and color photo/graphic/illustration would provide a momentary fresh breath of entertainment before digging into the next tragic historical scene.

Your book can be serious and strictly academic. Your book can be filled with comedic personal experiences and levity. In most cases, it will be a blend of both in what is or is about to become your signature style.

So as you are contemplating your perspective on this topic, think of what makes sense. If you tend to have a witty take on things, it might be difficult for you to put a very serious spin on a major human rights issue, for example. That's not to say you can't, but just as certain actors play certain types of roles, authors tend to write books that share similarities in perspective. The process will likely be less stressful as well as more enjoyable for you—and your intended audience—if you do what comes naturally.

My perspective when writing these books is that of a friend or mentor. I write these books for writers who don't necessarily need more information on how to put sentences together, but who are eager for someone to hype them up during what is one of the most lengthy and agonizing processes of a new writer's life: the first book.

As I am not the only author with this perspective, I need to follow through to make sure this book is distinctive. My goal is to figure out why someone would want to read this book over every other friendly nonfiction writing book. A lot of what makes a book successful is marketing, but at the end of the day, world-class marketing can't save a book that isn't worth reading.

But we're getting a little ahead of ourselves here. One of my more non-traditional perspectives is that I don't necessarily think you need to be published in order to enjoy writing a good book. I also believe we shouldn't be too tied to the concept of perfection as we write since that tends to dampen the enjoyment of the process. If you've read my previous books, you'll know that I'm a huge proponent of getting the book written first, then worrying about editing and revision.

That being said, you can't really edit from a new perspective. You can add and subtract facts. You can change your arguments a bit, as long as you have the supporting information you need. You can add all the adjectives and adverbs you know. But changing the perspective of a story mid-stream is going to undoubtedly generate some major rewrites.

Some people enjoy extra challenges. I do not. I like it best when things go well and come easily so I can enjoy doing them. Therefore, I encourage those who are trying their hand at nonfiction for the first time to check their perspective before they get started to make sure it fits and feels comfortable. Take a look at this quick exercise to help you figure out where you're going, and whether it's right for you.

Exercise: Check Your Perspective!

As a writer, one of the most common questions I'm asked is, "How do you decide what to write about?" Essentially, they're asking me how I choose my topic and refine my perspective. Since it can be a multi-layered process, I thought we'd try walking through the general concept together to see how it can work.

Sometimes, yes, the entire framework of a book floats down from the Muses, and it is beautiful. Other times, however, I need to do a little critical finagling with the Muses, my mind, and my readers. Let's try out a few of the methods I use when I'm working on a new book.

Supplies needed:

- *paper/writing utensil and/or open, blank .doc file, set to your preferences*

- *a solid chunk of quiet, uninterrupted time (I recommend an hour, but most of us don't have that kind of luxury regularly)*

- *Device to do online research, or your local library*

Step 1: What do you want to write about? Identify it in the least possible number of words.

Dolly Parton. How to Write a Billboard Hot 100 Hit. Your personal health journey. How wearing only leggings changed your life. Wakatomika, Ohio. Be as broad and non-specific as you can here.

Step 2: Why? What about it?

Here you start to refine your interest. Let me use the current book you are reading as an example yet again.

For Step 1, I came up with "How to Write Nonfiction." I've already done "how to write a book," and "how to write fiction," and I've gotten some feedback from nonfiction author hopefuls that they'd love more resources.

For Step 2, here are the notes that I jotted down (transcribed from a small notebook my friend gifted me that says "Tacos and Naps" on the cover—not everything has to be "official writer-grade"):

- They asked you to

  ○ Don't always do what they asked you to

  ○ Unless it's a good idea

WHAT DO YOU WANT EVERYONE TO KNOW ABOUT NON-FICTION???????

- Everyone says it's easy

- It's not easy—it's easy to write crap, but good non-fiction takes effort

- Many people don't know what that effort entails

  - Good topic

    - Needs to be interesting. Tell us why we care. Why should we read? Not too big, not too *(sic)* small. Look at things your way.

  - Put it together right

  - Make it sound good

  - How do I help people understand how to put a book together?

- There are so many non-fiction styles. Do I know them all?

  - History

  - How-to

  - Biography

  - Self-help

    - Research all of these so you don't sound lost- you know this stuff.

Holistic or broad?

— All n/f readers? Focus on style? Focus on writing a good book?

As you can see, my original inspiration for writing this book was the knowledge that there were at least a handful of people who thought it would be a good idea. As my notes clearly indicate, I realized very early this wasn't a good enough reason to commit myself to the entire task.

So I made myself pivot into my frustration at misconceptions about writing nonfiction. But then I started thinking about why I was frustrated, and I continued following myself down that rabbit hole.

Notice that I'm not doing any research here, but I'm making note of things I want to research. I actually have the word "research" highlighted in my original notes because I wanted to make sure I came back to that. You don't actually have to know everything there is to know about a topic before you decide to write a book about it. You just need enough interest and passion and an open mind to do the research to make it happen. When I started this book, I couldn't rattle off all of the different types of nonfiction. Obviously, I was familiar with them, but at that stage of the process, I wasn't a fine connoisseur of nonfiction. I wasn't even entirely sure about the difference between an autobiography and a memoir (don't fret, we'll talk about it).

At this stage, you may feel incredibly discouraged about your topic, depending on what you used to define "why" you want to write this book. There may not be a lot of notes there. There doesn't need to be a lot of notes there. Not yet. Don't despair—dig deeper. Tenacity is the key.

Step 3: Time to Research!

Let me preface this by saying you're not about to research the whole book at once. That would be madness. However, at this point, you may accidentally stumble upon some fantastic resources for future use. So whether you do this on an electronic device or wander through the shelves at your local library, find some way of saving your search history.

We're about to embark on a journey to help us see how this topic currently exists in the literary world. You can call it "sizing up the competition" or "finding your niche" or "market research" or whatever feels most appropriate to your personal approach to the matter. I like to say I'm "finding my place on the shelves," even though I know most folks read my books digitally.

Do a search for your topic as identified in Step 1 —Google or card catalog—and look at what comes up. In most cases, it's going to be thousands upon thousands of relevant selections. If you're writing an autobiography, memoir, or philosophical book, you may turn up very few hits. This is both a blessing and a curse because you have free rein to write everything you know... but you still have to do it just one book at a time.

Look back at your notes from Step 2. Search again for your topic, only narrow it down by adding terms that you clearly feel passionate about. I used terms like "nonfiction for new writers" and "what makes good nonfiction," for example.

I mention doing this search in a public library because "going analog" actually has the advantage here. If you want to know what has been written about pre-colonization agriculture in what is today known as New England, you can search a few different terms in the library's search system—formerly known as a "card catalog"—jot down a few different suggested options, then physically search the aisles and look at, pick up, and even read a bit from all of the recommended resources. The advantage over doing the same thing online is that you can actually see all of the books of similar topics right there in front of you without relying on an algorithm. You don't have to scroll. You can just move side to side and up and down and get a feel for the size, quality, and depth of different resources without clicking a bunch of different things.

However, I fully acknowledge that the method does not work for all writers or all topics. When writing this book, I was somewhat lost for search terms, so I felt like getting lost at the library would leave me feeling more anxious than inspired!

If you're doing this step online instead of or in addition to wandering the bookshelves, you may also want to check out some of the free SEO tools offered online for inspiration. "SEO" stands for "Search Engine Optimization," and many marketing professionals use these tools to help them understand what terms people are searching for and how often they're conducting these searches. These terms are known as keywords.

While this step will become important again if you decide to market your book for sale, right now you're just looking for keywords related to your ideas. I personally don't like to look too heavily at the keyword ranking—this is an indicator of how popular a search term is—unless I actually need a certain number of clicks, purchases, or downloads in order to be successful.

Instead, think of this as listening in to all of your potential readers telling you what really interests them. Find inspiration in the curiosity of others, and make it your goal to answer those questions and satiate those minds... whoever' they may be.

Step 4: Finding Your Readers

Speaking of your readers, another big influence in how you refine your perspective is figuring out who you're writing for... meaning, who is your audience?

This could be very broad- "young adult" or very specific- "young adults in the Midwest with an interest in livestock farming but not necessarily 4H." If you're trying to market your book for sale or shop for a publisher, you may want to be precise about your audience. If you just want to write for the sake of watching words appear on the page—which I do admit is very satisfying—then you might think about which of your friends and family members you would allow to read your book, if any. Your reader can be absolutely no one, in which case, you can skip this step entirely.

But, if you're interested in exploring this topic, there are a few different ways to narrow things down. If you've done an online SEO search, you may have discovered that keyword tools often have analytical functions that allow you to look at the demographics of who is searching for what. If you haven't gone online yet and you'd like to discover these fun tools, fear not—I've linked a few options in the Resources chapter.

Consider demographic research an insight into the readers' trains of thought. It's ok to compare it to your train of thought from Step 2, but don't start worrying about whether your idea is good enough or if you should change it to appeal to the masses. Instead, consider this a look at how others are approaching the topic to see how you may be able to refine your perspective. You don't have to take this information to heart but as more of a suggestion. You also don't have to drill down to the level of "What type of toothpaste do my readers use?" but rather, get a general idea of who shares your passion and interest in this topic. What's their education level? What other books do they read? What kind of music do they listen to? What's their level of social interaction like?

You may be wondering why all of this matters, and to some extent, it doesn't. I believe you should write whatever book your heart desires.

That being said, if you want people to read and enjoy your book, you're going to have to write your book in a way that they will *want* to read it and *easily* enjoy it. You will need to use words and concepts that they can understand. You will need to make references that are familiar to them. You want to write a book that doesn't leave your audience asking for a refund.

By knowing who your reader is, you can avoid overwhelming, angering, and confusing the people who choose to read your book. A kindergartener and a poet laureate are going to have very different vocabulary and reading comprehension skills, so choose who you're writing for and stick with it.

Step 5: Put It Together

Sometimes, I start this process and everything becomes crystal clear right away. I end up doing the research steps mostly to solidify my perspective and make sure I'm on the right path.

Sometimes, I do all the steps and I still have no clue what I'm doing. There are a few ways out of this:

1. **More research-** Rather than trying too hard to make things fit, intensify your research. I like to copy the link to each of my resources along with any interesting information found at that resource in a Google doc. Eventually, something will spark my interest, and hey! Didn't I see something about that back on that one site, a few clicks ago? It's really the definition of digging a deeper hole, but the likelihood of finding literary gold is pretty high. As you keep going, ideas, theories, questions, and opportunities will start to form in your mind. Nearly every time I've gone digging, I've found exactly what I was looking for—maybe it took a few days or weeks, but it was there.

2. **Adjust the topic**- There are no impossible topics. But maybe there really isn't very much interest *or* material out there to write about "Opossum UFO Encounters." But what about "Nocturnal Animals and Paranormal Experiences?" Maybe your topic really is too narrow or too broad, and rotating the kaleidoscope through which you view your topic ever so slightly will refocus your topic to meet your level of investment in writing this book.

3. **Adjust the audience**- If you're having a hard time figuring out how to write about your topic to certain folks, consider whether you're writing to the wrong crowd. There is an audience for everything, I assure you. Find your people. This may mean searching for social media or online communities that share your passion for your topic. I've actually done this a few times, and I met some very cool friends along the way!

4. **Delete, delete, delete**- I don't recommend this. You will regret this if only because you'll try to remember the references you looked at, and you'll never find them again because you deleted all of your notes. Keep the notes and become a valuable asset at Trivia Night.

As with any of my suggestions, I recommend you look at these steps and take away from it what you need. You don't have to do everything I say exactly. There is no "punishment" if you don't "do it right." In our world, that phrase is spelled "do it write," because as long as you are creating and feeling motivated and generally positive about the experience, you're on the right track. If at any time you read one of my exercises or suggestions and say "That's not how I'd do it," then I encourage you to do it exactly as you see fit. I'm a mentor, not a drill sergeant!

Be patient with yourself. I'm sure some writers are able to generate an idea while making their morning coffee and have the whole thing outlined by chapter by the time they finish breakfast. I'm not one of those people. I can't tell you how many times I've looked at the screen and thought "That will never work." I've even been right a few hundred times!

At the end of the day, there will be people who simply don't "get" your book. They'll find your sense of humor insufferable, and your style annoying, and they'll be more or less turned off by everything you've done to write your book. That's fine because you're not writing your book for that person.

Always write for yourself, but if you are interested in publishing, selling, or somehow sharing your book with others, consider carefully the ideas that came to mind and the things you discovered through this exercise!

Thoughtful Organization

Now that you have your topic and you know how you're going to explore it, it's time to consider how you're going to organize the book. While writing a stream-of-consciousness mind blurt of everything you are thinking can be very satisfying and a great way to get over a writer's block hump, it's not ideal for many nonfiction readers.

Furthermore, even if you are writing just for yourself and like the idea of a good stream-of-consciousness mind blurt, a thoughtful organization can make your life a lot easier. No matter the genre you pick, the topic you select, or the perspective through which you gaze, putting energy into organizing your book is never a bad idea.

First, a book is long. Even if you've got all of your ideas airtight and ready to go, you'll still likely need to stand up and stretch, go to the restroom, have a snack, and occasionally sleep while you're writing it. For most writers, 1,000-3,500 words is a pretty good day's writing session, but as I've said in my other books, don't hold yourself to this type of standard or you'll be miserable. How long it takes to write 1,000-3,500 words depends on how focused you are, how many interruptions you have, how many times you get lost in thought, how many times you have to look up synonyms and quotes, and so on. I have spent 8 hours on an assignment and walked away with 500 usable words for my efforts simply due to the amount of research I needed and my ability to concentrate.

What I'm trying to say is that a lot can happen in 1,000 words. You may not remember what has happened in the past 1,000 words. You may sit down tomorrow and not necessarily recall what you wrote two days ago. When you're writing, focused on a point, and trying to create a very big picture using very small-seeming words, you can become overwhelmed and forgetful.

Organization can keep you going in these difficult times. If you can refer to your notes and know exactly what you've already covered, you can skip the part where you repeat yourself *ad nauseam* and save yourself a lot of time and frustration.

Personally, I like to start with an outline. I know I'm going to have an Intro and a Conclusion, and that a Resources chapter is highly likely, so I start off with those. Then I look at the key areas I want to cover. For my goal of explaining the different types of nonfiction and how to explore them, I needed to figure out how to include them all. So, I grouped them:

1. Intro

2. ???

3. Biographies, Autobiographies, and Memoirs

4. History and Travel

5. Self-Help and How-To

6. Philosophy and Insight/Analysis

7. Conclusion

8. Resources

9. Intro

10. ???

11. Biographies, Autobiographies, and Memoirs

12. History and Travel

13. Self-Help and How-To

14. Philosophy and Insight/Analysis

15. Conclusion

16. Resources

So how did I figure out how to group them? That was probably the toughest part. Chapter 3 was perhaps the most obvious since those three genres are closely related. The rest required significant research.

I spent weeks looking into some of the top challenges experienced and discoveries made by professional writers while writing these topics. I dug into some of the uniting factors that can directly help guide writers who choose these genres, and grouped them by what we'll call "really important things to know." The challenges faced by self-help and how-to writers are often the same, so I put them together, for example. This will, of course, make more sense when you've read the chapters, but since we're using this book as an example of the process, bear with me for now.

Next, I started to make notes on what I wanted each chapter to contain:

6. Philosophy and Insight/Analysis

    1. Avoiding a stream-of-consciousness disaster

      a. HOW:

        i. Focus

        ii. Clarity

        iii. knowing the point you're trying to prove

    2. Make people care without holding them hostage or becoming a bully

These are the earliest, little, baby stages of chapters. Feel free to go back to the table of contents or flash forward to the chapter itself to see how this went, but suffice it to say, things have changed.

As I dove further and further into my research, I started making more and more connections between my initial impressions of how things would go and the reality of the facts. In this case, it was more of a fine-tuning exercise than a full rewrite, but I can assure you that you'll usually find yourself making notes in your outline, then using the cut/paste/rearrange method of putting related sources and points together until you've finally shuffled all the puzzle pieces into a working roadmap of your literary journey.

I am aware that there are many people out there who aren't big fans of outlines. I appreciate that, and I've mentioned a few alternative methods to outlining in my other books. What I want you to take away from this is that you have the ability to re-do and refine your book's organization as much as you need to until it feels "right."

I know some folks really enjoy the book template apps and software available for helping them get organized. I haven't actually tried any myself because I am old, cranky, and set in my ways, but I firmly believe that the best way for you to visualize your book is whatever system you develop. I know folks who use Magic Markers and multi-colored pieces of construction paper. Some writers just write everything down as it comes, potentially working on several different chapters each day. Then they reconstruct everything during editing and add whatever is needed to make these ideas flow.

If you have no idea where to start, try my outline idea. If you end up staring at a blank screen and a blinking cursor for more than 15 minutes, give up. Try writing an outline in a notebook. Do a vision board. Meditate about what it would take for you to visualize the order you want to work in. As long as you continue to feel inspired, excited, and not too terribly stressed, there is no wrong answer here.

Author's Note: Being Obvious

When it comes to writing some types of nonfiction, such as histories, biographies, and even some travel pieces, it's tempting to write things in chronological order. In fact, that's probably the easiest way for an author to organize many of these topics. It makes sense. Life happens chronologically, so you don't have to move things around in order to share your perspective with your audience.

If you feel this is the best way to present your ideas on your topic, then please proceed. But if you're trying to explain the "why" and "how" of something, you might need to draw on facts from around the world and across the expanse of history.

Let me simplify with an example. Let's say you're writing a book about how the development of dependable electricity in the United States has impacted the economy. One way to write this book would be to start with the dawn of the modern economy and how things were before the advent of electricity. Then you might look at the invention of electricity and the different areas that have benefited from it, such as manufacturing, communication, and agriculture. You might compare the influx of dependable electricity across the country with economic development over time, following the National Grid rollout.

OR! You could arrange the book by the different areas you wish to examine. One chapter can review pre-electricity manufacturing practices, what changed in the early 1900s when electricity came along, how practices have developed since then in direct relation to electricity becoming common, and the overall economic impact of those changes for mass production, market value, and so forth. The next chapter could be communication, starting with options prior to electricity, the changes, or how keeping in contact with others has now become an imperative part of social function and employment, and so on and so forth until you've examined all of the parts of the economy you wish to discuss.

As you can see, these are two very different books that include the same information. But as the writer, you get to choose how you present your facts. When doing so, please consider:

- *What do you want to read?*

- *What do you want to write?*

- *What do you think will really help each point you make stand out?*

- *Which will feel the most organic?*

Most readers don't read an entire book in one sitting, as much as we probably want to. As a result, readers generally don't like books that skip around too much. "In 1912, our hero went to Washington DC to discuss human rights, just as he had done in 1842, but this time was a little different." I strongly encourage you to consider how easy it is going to be for your reader to keep up with you when organizing your book, even if that means stepping away from the more obvious organization method and moving things around to make them more digestible.

Ultimately, staying organized as a writer will help your audience stay organized as a reader. Have you ever watched a movie in the theater, stepped out to use the restroom, returned, and had a brief moment of disorientation in which you thought you were in the wrong theater? The characters and scene changed so quickly, that your brief absence left you completely disoriented. This can happen to readers, too. Present information in a way that builds their knowledge, rather than throwing facts at them.

As writers, our relationship with our readers is complicated. On one hand, we have the ability to write any book we want about any topic, including all of our opinions, and put it together as well as the thoughts in our heads. On the other hand, if we want people to read our writing, we need to create something palatable for other people.

You get to choose who that audience is, and how many people you're willing to include in it. You are not limited in saying what you want about whatever you want, but there are consequences. If you head into defamation territory or start telling flat-out lies, then there's a possibility someone might sue you for libel.

Your readers also have the right to not like your book. Some of them won't understand it. I once signed up for a course during my undergrad days, only to open up the textbook and realize it made no sense to me. I dropped the class immediately. No one wants to suffer.

Only you can make the reading experience enjoyable and informative for your audience. If you spend some time selecting your topic, take care when whirling through the kaleidoscope of potential perspectives, and present your ideas in a meaningful, provoking, direct manner, you have a higher chance of making that happen.

Now, let's take a look at the various genres or styles that fit under the nonfiction umbrella, along with some special considerations to keep in mind when attempting your first foray into each!

BIOGRAPHIES, AUTOBIOGRAPHIES, AND MEMOIRS

E veryone has a story. Everyone has hopes, dreams, fears, opinions, theories, and ideas. Every life is a unique experience.

The stories of others can inspire us. Understanding how other individuals processed trauma and turmoil, discovered their talents, or made important decisions can give us insight into how these actions or reactions changed the entire world... or made a lasting impact on the individual experiencing them.

Biographies, autobiographies, and memoirs are nonfiction styles that share someone's life story. You may wish to write the entire life story of an individual, or in some cases, the history of a group of individuals, such as a band or a school of artists. You may wish to focus on your subject's specific contributions to history, art, science, technology, sports, or any other field. You may instead focus on their personal journey, or how their views developed over time based on events that occurred during their lifetime.

Your topic can be very well-known, or very personal. You could focus on how the Civil War impacted Abraham Lincoln's mental health, or you could explore how working the third shift has formed your sleeping and eating habits. You can write about yourself, someone you know, or someone you've never met. Whether they're in the here and now or the hereafter, any human experience can be the topic of a nonfiction book.

Biographies, autobiographies, and memoirs are our way of capturing the human experience, making sense of it, and sharing it with others. Though we may be writing about the life of another human being, we may never have the chance to actually interact with them. Therefore, the perspective of these books is purely our own.

As a result, it's often helpful to really nail down where you plan to go with these types of books before you get started, hence why I put them immediately following the chapter about planning and organizing your book! You can tell someone's life story in a series of short tales, like an elder relative may have shared stories with you, or go with a factual chronological account of events. Your goal is to share who that person is or was, and why and how their story can impact others. The choices you make surrounding the topic, perspective, and organization of the piece will undoubtedly influence the type of impact made, however.

One special consideration of biographies, autobiographies, and memoirs is the audience. Some of us lead rather, er, *sordid* lives, shall we say. That is to say, there are certain details about everyone's lives that we tend to avoid sharing with particular audiences. A book about Elvis written for a child in elementary school and for someone from the Boomer generation may have very different candid details, for example.

Furthermore, the amount of detail you might wish to include will vary between audiences. A more seasoned audience may be interested in the fine details of how and why Paul McCartney composed "And I Love Her," while in other instances, it may be more than enough to mention that this event happened at all.

All told, while every life is fascinating, not every detail is relevant. When writing biographies, autobiographies, and memoirs, it's a good idea to check yourself with how many important dates and events you wish to include compared to the points you're trying to make and the journey you're trying to share. If I were writing my own memoir, for example, I probably wouldn't include the fact that I had a Cabbage Patch doll drawn in icing on my third birthday cake, even though on that particular day, it meant the absolute world.

It is possible—and in some cases even imperative—to focus on a single era, time, or event in a person's life. You may wish to take a good, hard look at your topic and perspective to make sure it's going to give you enough room to explore without forcing you to write thousands of pages to express your ideas—unless that's your overall goal. But for those of us who are looking to write a modestly-sized book about something we enjoy, fine-tuning these areas will help you avoid burnout and keep you from abandoning your project.

The organization is also important in these types of books because it is very easy to get dates and events confused. Once you've written so many sentences like, "In June 1822, he turned 18. Shortly afterward, on July 18, his 22-year-old brother...", you'll find that your brain starts spinning a little. Having a solid system of organization can help you stop the spinning by focusing on real and true facts in an order that makes sense. This will also help you effectively meander through an entire lifetime of material to focus on the events that best support your ideas.

We'll look at many different things to keep in mind throughout this chapter, but as we're establishing each type of nonfiction and how to write it, I wanted to take the time to touch back to the points which can help you create a nonfiction book that you'll actually enjoy writing.

Read on to learn more about things to keep in mind when writing biographies, autobiographies, and memoirs.

What's the Difference?

If you're like me, the differences between a biography, an autobiography, and a memoir are some vague concepts that you understand but have never really needed to dive into... until the moment you absolutely do.

As a writer, it's a good idea to keep yourself educated about writing, but no human being is expected to know the intimate nuances of every technical aspect of their career. That's why references and resources exist. In that spirit, let's take a look at biographies, autobiographies, and memoirs, each in more detail, so you can decide which option is best for your big book idea.

Biographies

Of the three, a biography is the most easily recognizable and definable. This is the story of a person or sometimes people, as told by you. The subject can be absolutely anyone—from a cultural icon to your next-door neighbor—as long as it isn't yourself.

There are many reasons why someone might choose to write a biography. They may wish to connect an individual's life experiences to their contributions to society. Perhaps the biography is intended to reveal that person's personality or outlook. A biography can focus on struggles, triumphs, or a bit of both.

It's also possible to write a biography about multiple people. Earlier, I gave examples of a musical band or a school of artists, but you can also write a biography about an entire community of people, like the settlers of Roanoke or the underground gambling market of New York City.

When writing about multiple people, you'll want to be careful about how much you focus on each individual. In some cases, such as writing about ancient civilizations, you won't have too many specific details about each and every individual. On the other hand, if you're writing about a famous music group, you might have more details than you know what to do with at first.

Most biographies include the following details:

- Name of a person or people (Frank Sinatra, The Anasazi culture, Corvette enthusiasts)

- Information about that person's birth, or establishment of a group of people (born in *place* on *the date*, fossils indicate roamed the area in *a year*, founded by *a person* in *a year*)

- Their personal life (upbringing, family life, and relationships)

- Their educational experiences (school, oral and written traditions, practical experience in a field)

- What they did (life events, achievements, and challenges)

- Why they are important in their field, to a group of people, or society as a whole

They can also include:

- Interviews and introspection

- Theories as to their motivation, inspiration, or purpose

- Media or scandals surrounding the subject

- Analysis of their overall impact in their field, to a group of people, or society as a whole

You can approach a biography from many directions. You can paint your subject as a hero, as a villain, or neutrally. I mentioned earlier that you'll want to have a certain sense of passion for your project, but that can mean any type of enthusiasm or energy you have about discussing the topic. It is not unheard of for someone to write a biography that critiques or disparages the actions and decisions of the subject.

You can also choose to be as "safe" or illicit in your portrayal as you wish—as long as you remember your audience. When writing about Madonna, for example, I could have taken the route of exploring her more risque performances and publications, but it wasn't the right audience. Instead, I tried to write the story people didn't expect—a heartwarming tale of a woman who grew up motherless and longed to become a mother. I felt my audience was less interested in rehashing the sensational news stories and more interested in understanding who Madonna is as a person.

As you start the process of choosing your biography topic and perspective, consider what story you're going to tell. Who are you sharing this story with, and what do you hope for them to learn from this? We'll get a little more into the research and writing process for biographers in the next chapter, but for now, I recommend taking your time when getting organized to make sure you've got a well-established plan before you get started.

Autobiographies

Autobiographies, on the other hand, tell the story of one very specific person: you.

An autobiography may be written in the first person or as a third-person narrative, but the main subject is always the author themself. Regardless of the style or perspective, an autobiography is always a self-portrait.

The content of an autobiography is generally the same as a biography, including your birth, early life, education, job experiences, as well as the pinnacles and pratfalls you have experienced to date.

At first glance, this seems like a super-easy task. After all, we have an innate expertise in our own insights and motivations. You don't actually need to do any research, right?

Well, kind of. See, you still need to have a perspective, and you might want to pare down your topic a bit to focus on a particular facet of your life. But writing an autobiography means having to reflect on the events of your life. You may need to look up dates. You may wish to interview people who were there for these specific times to get their angle on the situation. You might want to tie in current events, which means creating a timeline and getting a feel for what those events entailed, and why it's important for you to reflect upon them.

But most of all, you want to be organized. We'll talk a little bit more about what writing a book about yourself entails, but think of how frequently your thoughts go bouncing around when you open the "Halls of Memory". How do you decide how much context to

include, and how many "scenes" to include? Again, we'll get to that
bit in a part, but keep it in mind that most autobiographies are not
merely a writer jotting down, "Here's what I thought today and what
I think it means." That's more of a philosophical type of book, which
we'll explore in a few chapters.

At the core of the organization is often the "why" of book writing.
As we discussed several times in Chapter 1, writers of "good" nonfiction ask themselves why they're doing what they're doing many, many
times. Sometimes it's more of a moaning curse, but we're looking at
"why am I writing this book" from the standpoint of "what are my
intentions for writing this book, who do I want to read it, and what
do I hope they are going to gain from it."

There are many reasons to want to tell your story:

- Because of your contributions to society

- Because you overcame a struggle and wish to inspire others

- Because you happen to need a little money and you have
  some information to share

- Because your side of a very important story needs to be told

- Because your story is your legacy that you wish to share with
  future generations

- Because you simply feel like it

Any of these, or others, is a valid reason to start the writing process,
but again, I urge you to take into consideration how much it means
to you that other people read and enjoy this book. You don't have to
have a reason to tell a tale, but you do have to make some kind of point

while doing it, or else the readers will feel confused and betrayed, as discussed earlier.

Paying close attention to your autobiography's organization can ensure that you maintain a grip on your intended audience throughout your tale, as they'll be able to follow you easily along the trail you've blazed.

Memoirs

Some people use the terms "autobiography" and "memoir" interchangeably, and that's... sort of true. Much like the relationship between the rectangle and the square, a memoir is always an autobiographical piece, but not every autobiography can be considered a memoir.

Memoirs typically focus on a specific event, time period, or facet of a person's life, such as their struggle with mental health in high school, that one time when they launched a new app that sold millions, or their experiences with the loss of a loved one.

Like autobiographies, they're typically told in the first person—but not always. Also like autobiographies, they can include information like your name, experiences growing up, education, and career stats. But unlike autobiographies, they focus most on a particular experience or set of events and include the actions, reactions, and emotions of that time period. It may include how things were before the catalyst of your book, as well as how things are now, but unlike an autobiography, a memoir is a rumination on a very specific topic or event within your life.

I mentioned earlier that a finely-tuned topic frequently has a more specific audience, and that notion is sustained in the spirit of the memoir. Whether the tone of your memoir is triumphant or traumatic, you'll need to decide who you want to read this book as you're putting together your notes. Are you writing for people who are now in your shoes, experiencing the same things you've survived, or are you writing for those who have someone in their lives who has faced these things? Are you providing education for people who aren't familiar with the challenges and triumphs you've been through? The way you frame your story and the level of personal detail you include may vary depending on who you want to read your book.

Ultimately, when you are writing a biography, autobiography, or memoir, you are taking on the responsibility of presenting an actual human being's life to your audience. The art of representation is monumental—especially if you're writing about yourself. Let's take a look at how you can use research and writing techniques to really let your audience know about your subject.

How to Talk about Someone You May Not Know

Personally, I get nervous about writing biographical pieces, especially if the person I'm writing about is still alive. That means there's a chance they'll read it. What if they aren't impressed, or worse yet, threaten to sue me?

Thankfully, that hasn't happened to date, and I believe it's because I take extreme care to write about these individuals. I write as though I am ghostwriting their autobiography, taking care to highlight the things they're passionate about and being fair and fact-based when discussing any controversy.

Of course, you may not be interested in painting your subject in a warm light. Critical pieces are just as important as praise, and sordid lives are often the most entertaining. These are the pieces that are more likely to ruffle some feathers.

When you're writing a biography, you *must* research to avoid legal entanglements. There are two specific reasons for this:

1. Libel is the publication of writing, pictures, cartoons, or any other medium that exposes a person to public hatred, shame, disgrace, or ridicule, or induce an ill opinion of a person, and are not true.

Actions for libel result mainly from news stories that allege crime, fraud, dishonesty, immoral or dishonorable conduct, or stories that defame the subject professionally, causing financial loss either personally or to a business (Associated Press Style and Libel Guide 251).

1. Defamation is a statement that injures a third party's reputation. The tort of defamation includes both libel (written statements) and slander (spoken statements). State common law and statutory law govern defamation actions, and each state varies in its standards for defamation and potential damages. Defamation is a tricky area of law as the lines between stating an opinion versus a fact can be vague, and defamation tests the limits of the first amendment freedoms of speech and press (https://www.law.cornell.edu/wex/def amation).

The phrase "defamation is a tricky area of law" is enough to stop me in my tracks. I, personally, do not wish to be embroiled in any sort of legal case. I don't want to hire a lawyer. I don't want to be sworn in or cross-examined. I want to write books, have fun, and get paid.

Therefore, I make it a point to carefully vet all of my resources. Most of the time, it's pretty easy to do so with a single click. I know you're not supposed to judge a book or a webpage by its cover, but if I find myself on a site laden with Blingees, last updated in August 2006, it isn't a bad idea to doubt its veracity.

As writers, we also have the ultimate "get-out-of-jail-free card," which is citing our resources. Phrases like "According to (resource)," or "The story told about this event in (resource)," can be very helpful for exposing the fact that you did not invent this information, but are merely drawing conclusions based on what others have published. Of course, it's a good idea to cite your resources anyway because plagiarism is an actual sin. Quoting, on the other hand, is good for back-link SEO, not to mention the soul.

Bear in mind that there are many different types of resources, as well. Most of us tend to start looking up books and conducting Google searches, but those aren't the only possible sources. One fun element unique to biographies is the chance to conduct interviews, either with your subject or other experts on your subject, such as family members, historians, archaeologists, and experts in your subject's field. Look for published diaries or journals, television or audio recordings, and transcripts, too.

I'd like to take a deeper dive into what it means to vet your resources since this can be so crucial to aspiring biographers. It can mean the difference between a compelling, well-received book and a mistake-laden flop.

Author's Note: The Difference between Accurate and Anecdotal

Technology is a godsend for writers. We have all sorts of devices that can record everything we say or do, so we can play them back and accurately describe and transcribe the scene. However, technology hasn't always been around. Sometimes we have to rely on how other people have described and transcribed these scenes.

You've probably heard the phrase from Robert Evans: "There are three sides to every story: your side, my side, and the truth." Meaning, there's the perspective of Person 1, the perspective of Person 2, and the actual, factual account of the situation. To make things even more complicated, frequently everyone who is in any way impacted by, adjacent to, or knew someone who knew someone in connection to a notorious person will come out of the woodwork to share their thoughts. I'm not saying they are necessarily liars, but we frequently embellish or misremember things when we're excited or nervous, which most of us are when we're being interviewed.

Anything you read that is not a verbatim transcription of an interview, speech, or conversation will be considered anecdotal. Even a person recalling an experience may not remember exactly what they said, or the specific order of events, especially if it wasn't particularly important to them at that moment. Do you recall the exact words you said when you learned how to ride a bicycle for the first time? Or which sock you put on first on the day you met your partner or spouse? You may remember that you shouted, or that you were wearing socks with cats on them, but some of the details fall off with time and more important events.

Generally speaking, if this anecdotal information is considered valid—meaning it's been published or otherwise approved or licensed by the individual or their estate—then it's not very risky to use it.

The only way to be fully accurate is to use original recordings, diaries, letters, or notes from the party involved. This can get a little sketchy if you're working with subjects who are long deceased because the interpretation and translation of what they said, wrote, or painted on cave walls will be subject to the perspective of the interpreter.

Unfortunately, the only way to write a completely accurate account of a person's life is to interview them directly, which may or may not require the invention of time travel. What we can do, however, is treat anecdotes for what they are: the best possible retelling we have. Wording like, "In his 1980 interview, (subject's) childhood friend Bill stated that..." or "Newspaper accounts at the time stated that (subject)...." You can only tell the truth as it is reported to the masses.

Also on the table is the semi-fictional take on a person's life, known as "biographical fiction." While the events portrayed in the writing are true, perhaps we don't know exactly who was present, or exactly what words were spoken. For example, we're not entirely sure where everyone was sitting during the signing of the Declaration of Independence, but if you're writing about the scene, you may need to have Benjamin Franklin tap Thomas Jefferson on the shoulder to make a point. We don't necessarily know whether that actually happened, but it's reasonable to think that it could have. It's also not incendiary or potentially defamatory.

This style is common among historical and biographical works intended for younger readers, though it's certainly not limited to any particular age group.

Generally speaking, biographical fiction is shelved with other works of fiction, but given the intense overlap with nonfiction, I wanted to give it a call-out. Everything in this book can apply to writers of semi-fictional biographical or historical pieces as well.

When writing a biography, understanding the difference between accurate and anecdotal resources can be helpful in avoiding trouble later, with your audience or your subject.

Regardless of whether you plan to paint a rosy portrait of your subject or share your overwhelming disapproval of them, it's important to most writers to talk about other people in a way that will not impact them legally. You don't have to be nice, of course—you just have to avoid making things up. Choosing your resources carefully and understanding the difference between accurate and anecdotal information can help you with that endeavor.

In a nutshell, when you're talking about other people, it's a good idea to make sure your vision for your book aligns with the resources you have. A highly clinical book is going to need more accurate resources, but by framing and presenting anecdotal information as just that, you can avoid legal and reputational calamity.

An Actual Anecdotal Biographical Piece for Your Consideration:

Perhaps the best advice I can give you is what I learned from a professor in college. Though the topic of the course wasn't specifically about publishing, we students would sometimes wheedle our professor into discussing and describing his trials and tribulations in being published. I'll preserve his anonymity simply because it's been decades since we've lost touch, but suffice it to say, he was a well-recognized author who had received many prestigious awards, and I was lucky to study under him.

When it came to biographies, his advice was to treat the subject with respect. Even if we hated our topic with unwavering passion, he recommended we give a biographical subject—alive or deceased—respect as a living being. It's best to use your words to describe why they are such a horrible person—don't attempt to invent anything or go with low-blow insults. If written well, a nonfiction piece can reveal exactly how the writer feels about a certain topic without resorting to name-calling or toeing the line of libel. Don't put words in your subject's mouth—let them do all the talking.

You may or may not disagree with this particular advice, but it's certainly something to keep in mind when you're writing about someone else. You don't have to say your worst enemy is the best guy you've ever met, but you also don't have to refer to him as "that stupid idiot" in every paragraph.

But what if you do know the person you're writing about? The chance to actually interview a person about their experiences is one of my favorite things about nonfiction because you can actually tune in to their telling and understand events and circumstances through their first-hand account. But, it can also be a bit nerve-wracking to know that the person you're writing about will, in fact, be checking in on what you've said.

I strongly encourage you to record whatever interview sessions you have, whether that be an audio or video recording. Remember that you need to get permission before recording someone, but if the individual is aware and accepting of the fact that you're writing about them, that's generally not hard to do.

Personally, when I'm writing about someone with whom I've actually interacted, I like to try to capture the overall vibe of speaking with them. What is their body language like as they recount their tales? Do they have certain inflections in their voice or little mannerisms that are noteworthy?

Not only does painting the picture of your subject help invite the reader into the situation, but it can also actually make the writing process a little easier. For most of us, writing about a real, tangible scenario that we have actually encountered is a little more familiar and comfortable than writing about something completely foreign to our experiences. Visual artists have used models for portraits since the dawn of creation, so it's really no surprise that literary artists should do the same. Plus, it's really nice to be able to email or phone your subject to clear up any questions you might have.

Alas, writing a biography about a living person in your sphere of existence isn't always possible. That being said, it is entirely possible to use some of the techniques you would use when interviewing a subject while doing your research.

For example, you might have very specific questions for George Washington, and while it's impossible to communicate with him via traditional means, you can still ask those questions. Instead of posing them over the phone or in person, you'll have to answer them by conducting a lot of research. Forming specific questions that are pertinent to your topic and perspective and finding the answers for them can be a great way to refine your research and help you choose resources that will actually help you, rather than repeat all of the things you've already learned.

Writing a biography can be a complicated, anxiety-inducing experience, but you can gain control of the fear by gathering adequate, accurate resources and bringing a bit of basic respect to the table. When in doubt, stick to the facts, and let your words express your emotions. This is true of all types of writing, particularly when you're actively avoiding legal consequences.

Next, let's look at how to speak warmly and accurately about and not defame yourself... and yes, that is kind of a thing.

How to Talk About Yourself

At first glance, the idea of talking about yourself may seem pretty simple. After all, you were there, you have a generally good idea of what you said and what happened, so you should be able to describe events and conversations in detail, right?

There are two slight hiccups in this idealistic view of autobiographies and memoirs, however.

First, there's that thing about multiple perspectives and individual views. Everyone who has a memory of an event remembers it from their own perspective, as mentioned earlier. One interesting example of this phenomenon is the conversations that occur when you ask someone where they were on the date of a major event. Common examples include "when JFK was assassinated," or "on 9/11," not that the actual events have to be significantly tragic. If you survey your family about where they were when Aunt Helen dropped the birthday cake in the swimming pool, you'll get the same rousing round of different perspectives.

Then there's the traditional unreliability of memory itself. I'm not attempting to insult your IQ or your memory, but most of us lack 100% recall. With all due respect, most folks don't have the full picture, even if they were the subject of the portrait. It's not that we're lying to ourselves or anyone else, but that our brains are weird things that remember whatever they want to remember.

For example, we may remember the idea of what someone said or the emotional content of what they said rather than the exact words themselves. When recounting incidents out loud, we may narrate them with phrases like, "Then he said something about how I didn't need another pair of shoes. And I pointed out that he has, like, 500 pairs of shoes himself, and then he was just, UGH." This is clearly not a verbatim conversation. And, unless you specifically memorized the entire conversation, any attempt you have to repeat it word-for-word will result in your brain filling in some of the gaps with what it under-stood, rather than the actual words used.

So, given that our memories are more anecdotal than accurate, how can we trust ourselves to write an autobiography or a memoir?

I personally recommend being candid with your readers, as you would with any anecdote. In the autobiographical piece *Slash*, by Anthony Bozza and Slash of Guns 'n' Roses, the guitarist admits several times that the tale is told through his own lens and that others who witnessed certain events might have their own version to share.

Alternately, you can "screw your courage to the sticking place" and proceed with full confidence that you know exactly what you said, and you're willing to stand by it. Don't back down, and grit through any self-doubt with belief in your memories.

For the most part, this can only be troublesome if you start making up blatant lies about yourself. We live in the internet age, and it doesn't take too many keystrokes to discover that you did not, in fact, direct, write, and produce the blockbuster movie *Titanic*. Unless, of course, you are James Cameron, these are simply untrue claims.

There is a certain amount of humility that comes with writing about yourself. Sure, you have the power to spin and manipulate any conversation you've had into something that paints you as a hero. You can spend all the pages you wish justifying why you said what you said or did what you did. In fact, some people write memoirs for this exact purpose.

I can't dissuade anyone from putting on rose-colored glasses before they write about themselves, but consider how redecorating the "Halls of Memory" can benefit your reader. If you wash away all the stains of conflict, you might walk away looking pretty spiffy. But will your readers really understand the struggle and the lesson learned? No one really wants to read a book about things going really well all the time. They want the cathartic experience of tension building and being released. They want to learn lessons and understand things from a new perspective. Sure, they're interested in hearing about great people, but don't we all crave the truth? And sometimes, the truth gets a little gritty.

Before you commit to writing an autobiography or a memoir, ask yourself if you're ok writing about the things you may not love about your life. Are you ok with people you don't know reading about these things? What about people you do know, who may not be as familiar with those particular details of your life? If you feel any hesitation or reservation about these things, then maybe it's not time to write about it yet.

Many people write about themselves in order to share something they've gone through, either to give hope to others or to help themselves truly process the events and what they've learned as a result. When I share my personal experiences as a writer with you, I'm doing so to demonstrate that I've been in your position before, and to show you the roadmap of how I got through that particular challenge. I also recognize that most of my notes and early writing steps are messy, semi-incoherent, and often riddled with typos and errors. I could tidy that up before I commit it to the screen, but I prefer not to because I want you to appreciate that ugliness is part of the process. So many of us are caught up in the concept that we must do everything perfectly the first time, and that's simply impossible in writing. Rather than burn out on your first book trying to make things just right, I encourage you to slop around until you find your footing. If I show you my sloppiness, I hope that it makes you feel more comfortable with your own.

If your autobiographical piece includes some ugliness, be sure you're ready for it by preparing your notes. You are your own best resource here, but you can interview others. You can include actual historical events. You can paint yourself however you wish, but you can't make things up. And you're definitely going to make mistakes, but you have every chance to learn from it and come out of it looking not like a hero, but like someone readers can relate to.

To get a feel of how awkward or easy writing about yourself can be, let's give it a whirl for this chapter's writing exercise!

Exercise: 15 Minute Memoir

The premise of this exercise is exactly what it sounds like we're going to take 15 minutes out of our day to write a memoir.

As with exercises in my previous books, I'll be doing this alongside you and sharing what I came up with when I tried it myself. This means you get to read raw, unedited mind drivel in hopes that it will inspire you to make your own mess out of letters and words!

Supplies needed:

- *paper/writing utensil and/or open, blank .doc file, set to your preferences*

- *15 minutes of uninterrupted time*

- *optional - a timer to keep track of time*

As we just discussed, a memoir is an autobiographical piece that focuses on a specific event or occasion. That means you're going to spend the next quarter hour writing about one particular memory.

Step 1: Pick a Memory

I recognize that not everyone who is reading this book is absolutely sold on writing their own memoir, so let me give you a handful of topics to choose from:

- Your first day at a new school

- The first time you met your significant other

- A vacation or trip that you enjoyed a great deal

- Your favorite way to spend a summer afternoon

- A time when something embarrassing happened in front of

your coworkers

• The first time you ____ (anything!)

For the purpose of this exercise, you don't necessarily have to make a major revelation or educate the audience. I encourage you to choose a topic that you'll feel comfortable brainstorming and writing about for the next 15 minutes. Don't choose anything emotional or that will require a deep-dive into your psyche for this particular exercise—save that for the main event!

Step 2: Gather Your Wits

Before you get started, I recommend setting yourself up for success. This means setting a timer, getting your writing area organized, jotting down a few notes to help you keep on track, and placing a glass of water within convenient reach but not so close that you'll knock it over and interrupt yourself.

Close the doors, lower the blinds, tell everyone in your household to leave you alone, and get ready to write. If you need headphones or sound, make it happen now.

Step 3: Take a Deep Breath and Write

Clear your mind of any noise. Don't worry about messing up. Remember no one is going to actually read this. This is not a race. Don't worry about word count or typos. I'm not judging you.

Start the timer if you choose to have one, buckle up, and write.

Step 4: Stop and Read What You Wrote

Some writers—myself included—have to read what they've written immediately once they've stopped, or they'll never read it at all. It's really easy to assume that you've written something absolutely awful and procrastinate about reading it until you're so mortified by its existence, you delete it before you can read it and realize it really wasn't that bad.

Other folks like to take a break away from what they've just written so they can get out of their own heads. They reset their brain by focusing on something else so they can casually and peacefully approach their own material.

When it feels appropriate for you, take a look at what you came up with in those 15 minutes. Here's my effort, which should encourage you that perfection is not at all the point of this exercise:

My Very First Day of Kindergarten

When I attended kindergarten, it was still a half-day affair. You either joined the big kids on the bus in the morning when it was still dark and gray, or you got on the half-sized bus that cruised through the neighborhood on what we called "Baby Duty," dropping off the AM Kindergarten kids and picking up the afternoon shift.

I don't remember whether I was an AM or PM kid. I think it was afternoon, but I don't specifically remember. I do, however, remember that I stayed awake almost the entire night before my first day of kindergarten because I had no idea how this was going to shake out, and that made me feel scared.

My parents had informed me that if I was looking for someone to play with, a girl named Mindy would be a good choice because she lived in the neighborhood. That meant we could play more often. I asked why I hadn't met Mindy yet if she just lived up the street. My parents said I had, and I just didn't remember it.

It was still a few months from my fifth birthday when I started kindergarten. I had to take special tests and meet with people at the government buildings downtown. The tests were kind of fun—I had to think about the answers a bit. Talking to a bunch of strange grownups wasn't as much fun, but my parents told me it was ok to talk to them, so it wasn't exactly scary, either.

Whenever I finished a test or talked to someone, I got some paper and pens so I could draw for a bit. Unfortunately, this was the 1980s, so while my still-developing brain dreamed of creating an awe-inspiring portrait of Rainbow Brite, it was executed in standard office pen colors of red, green, blue, and black. I wondered why adults would bother being adults if they couldn't even draw in colors. "Maybe they should have crayons," I pondered as I scribbled my way through yet another juvenile noir take on a popular cartoon. I hoped kindergarten had crayons.

Kindergarten did, in fact, have crayons. It had bins upon bins of dusty halves and quarters of mutilated crayon stubs. Unlike the brand-new set of 36 that rested securely in a pocket strapped behind my seat, these abandoned nubbins were not organized by color, and while you could find a surprise like magenta or teal in there, it wasn't guaranteed. There was a distinct possibility that you might be coloring in your entire page in shades of yellow and green. These were, in my personal estimation, the worst colors. Blue, purple, and orange were the best.

My kindergarten teacher was an actual saint of a grandmotherly woman. In my eyes, she was older than all of my grandparents combined. In reality, she was probably in her late 50s. She helped us find our seats and explained all of the different things in the classroom to us, and finally, finally, just before we were to go home, I got to meet Mindy.

As you read whatever arose to the surface of this exercise, ask yourself a few questions about what you wrote.

- Were you surprised by what memories you decided to focus on?

- Was this harder than you expected, or easier?

- Did you struggle to recall any particular facts?

- Do you think you could keep writing on this topic? (If so—go for it!)

For me, I was surprised by the fact that I remember how scared I was. I was fine with the idea of school, and even though I wasn't a socially-inclined child, I knew how to entertain myself. It just felt like a really big commitment to something I didn't fully understand. It was interesting to see my brain walk through the process of how I became a kindergartner in this exercise.

The hardest part was trying to set the scene. I found myself writing as though I was talking to a kindergarten-aged me to give it a juvenile, simple feel. I would definitely edit this piece to more fully reflect that voice if I were to continue it. With more than 15 minutes at my disposal, I would have given more consideration to the voice and committed to it fully from the first word.

I couldn't remember whether I was an AM or PM kid. In fact, I probably spent at least one of my fifteen allotted minutes trying to remember. Consider this an argument for getting organized and coming up with ideas before you start writing because I could've used that minute to advance the actual story more.

I could probably keep writing about this, but I'd need to pare down the topic a bit more. Am I going to talk about how hard it was to establish new friendships? The frustrations of being an only child in a room filled with children who didn't share my passion for neatness and organization? A social piece on how we deprive office workers of creativity by only offering four basic colors of pen?

What I'm hoping to demonstrate with this exercise is all of the many things we've discussed in this chapter—from understanding the notable "characters" of biographical pieces to appreciating specific challenges that can arise when writing each type. I also hope you have an idea of how those concepts of choosing a shiny new topic, fine-tuning your perspective, and remaining organized can help you as you dive into your book.

You'll want to continue to keep these points in mind as we check out what it takes to write historical and travel-oriented books. Though the topics are very different, you are taking yourself out of your current context in order to write about people, times, and places that you may never experience firsthand. Some of what we have discussed about biographies will continue to serve you as we write about places, both in time and on the map.

HISTORY AND TRAVEL

B oth history and travel books are types of nonfiction that ask us to hop across dimensions in order to write our book. Though it is certainly possible to visit historic places, and travel destinations are limited by your budget and bravery, most historical and travel-related nonfiction are written from the viewpoint of someone who is currently in the time and place they are writing about.

There are, of course, exceptions. You may choose to write a travel diary, in which you capture your thoughts and actions while you are "on location," so to speak. Some could also argue that a diary is more of a memoir than a travel piece, which goes back to my carlier statement about nonfiction genres frequently blending and becoming a bit confusing.

For the sake of this chapter, we'll consider "historical pieces" as those which follow a specific event, a period in time, or developmental process. Examples could include: "The Day Mount Vesuvius Erupted", "The Building of Native American Ceremonial Mounds in the Midwest", or "The Evolution of the Ford Mustang."

Travel pieces can have a lot of range, too, depending on your definition of "travel." Some writers focus on a particular location—let's use
my father's hometown of Pawtucket, Rhode Island as an example. A
book about Pawtucket could include a history of the location, notable
residents, industry and commerce, places to eat, unique places to visit,
local folklore and flavor, and nearby points of interest. It could also
focus on a specific type of travel, such as "romantic getaways" or "fun
for the whole family." You could even toe the line of history and
write about what residents of Pawtucket did for fun between 1940
and 1970.

Other writers choose to highlight the process of traveling. Kristine
Hudson is an author I admire greatly. Her books dance on the line
between travel and how-to as she explains how she and her husband
quit their jobs to live and work in a van. Your travel book may reflect
on what you should pack, what to look for in an ideal vacation desti-
nation, when to choose side trips, and how to relax while getting ready
to travel.

Then again, there's the experience of travel. Think of travel writer
greats like Anthony Bourdain, who traveled the world to understand
cultures through their cuisine, or Bill Bryson, who simply went for "A
Walk in the Woods" and emerged with a best-seller. These writers take
readers along for the journey, but they also pause and reflect on what
their adventures mean, mentally, physically, and emotionally. While
these books may have step-by-step guidebook elements, they often
cross into autobiographical and memoir territory with their deep,
introspective reflection.

There can even be an interplay between historical and travel-based
pieces. If you're writing about a particular location, it's often helpful
to get into historical notes when explaining points of interest. Let's
say you're writing about things to do in Gettysburg. Aside from being

a lovely spot in Pennsylvania, the battlefields are a significant part of local and American history. Someone writing a guide to the location would have a hard time avoiding a discussion about the Civil War and the importance of the "High Water Mark of the Rebellion."

Similarly, if you're discussing the history of a particular place, you might investigate what that place is really like. Every event occurred somewhere, and setting the scene is pretty important, as we'll discuss in a bit. For example, a book about Mount Vesuvius may include notes about places impacted by the eruption, such as Pompeii and Herculaneum. A description of the Italian coastline and where these places lie in relation to the volcano can help readers appreciate the impact of the eruption.

This is already a lot to think about, but rest assured that we're going to dive a lot deeper into creating your own historical or travel pieces. Take your time digesting this, and when you're ready, read on to take a look at some of the special considerations that writers of history and travel nonfiction may want to keep in mind.

Recognizing Rabbit Holes

When we are passionate about something, we tend to obsess about it. When we obsess about things, we often direct our energy into learning as much as possible and/or surrounding ourselves with the object of our passion. We build on our personal resources, developing our passion with knowledge. And just as every kettle needs to blow steam when it boils, we absolutely adore sharing our expertise when appropriate.

Great news! There is no time more appropriate than when you are writing your very own book about your favorite topic! However, just because you have a captive audience does not mean you should take this opportunity to hold them, hostage.

All writers explore rabbit holes—I'd say anyone with a certain level of curiosity is game to chase a concept through its entirety. If you've read *Alice's Adventures in Wonderland*, you may be familiar with what happens when you chase white rabbits down holes. While Alice truly did have an amazing experience, remember that she didn't enjoy all of it, and she encountered quite a bit of danger along the way. While you may be comfortably typing away in your seat, your future audience does not necessarily want to be taken on a wild ride.

Alternately, they may very much wish to go on a wild ride, but in a controlled and coherent sort of way. As the author, it is your responsibility to keep the reader entertained and informed, which means you have the power to wander through as many rabbit holes as you feel will help you explain your point. If there are too many rabbit holes, the infrastructure collapses, and if there are too few, your story will feel like a lateral shuffle through facts. Even scientific studies share related data and provide context.

Ultimately, your decision of what to include or not include in your book goes all the way back to the very first step, when you chose your shiny topic. In practice, however, you will find many shiny things along the way, and throughout your research, you might start to follow other authors' rabbit holes and get caught up in your own Wonderland adventure.

All types of nonfiction offer their own opportunities for intrepid researchers to get completely lost, disoriented, and re-routed. For some, this is a huge, distracting consumer of valuable time.

I don't want to say it's a "waste of time" because I feel we're never wasting time when we're learning and growing as human beings. However, I can say from experience that writing a book requires a certain level of energy. And while finding a new thread to research will provide fascination and a significant burst of endorphins, you may feel something akin to regret when you realize that you've spent all of your designated writing energy reading about something that really doesn't have anything to do with your book.

For some writers, though, this temporary lapse of focus is a blessing, because that rabbit hole led them away from their intended topic and into a new realm that's far more inspiring. Others, however, may be far too committed to their topic to switch gears and rearrange everything. I have experienced both of these scenarios, and they can be very emotional for so many reasons. I do recommend, if you find a particularly delicious diversion, to go ahead and take notes. Copy the resources so you can come back and possibly wrangle another book out of it. At the very least, you'll know where to start when you have time to research for fun again.

If you do decide to start over with this new information, I would also encourage you to not delete what you have so far. Your exploration thus far led you to this place, so it's possible you'll need to know how to make that journey again. Consider your research thus far a road map to opportunity, and save it for future voyages.

While all types of nonfiction are prone to writers diverging from the topic momentarily, historical

and travel pieces are particularly fertile grounds for off-topic exploration. My own theory is that there is simply such an abundance of moving pieces to analyze when you're looking at a historical event or describing something as generally exciting as travel. With so many glittering perspectives vying for your attention, it is very easy to get distracted by a particular element of your topic.

Again, this goes back to the stage where you worked to establish your perspective. This is why I recommend doing a lot of research at that stage before you jump in wholeheartedly. The more you feel comfortable with your topic and perspective, the less likelihood you'll have of encountering a new view that you'd rather explore. Not to say that hasn't happened to me many times, but sometimes it's less of a shock and more of a begrudging acceptance that your original topic wasn't as stellar as you thought.

What about research? Your research will help inform what you include in your nonfiction book, so you might want to pay close attention to how much your research and your book outline match. If you find yourself going off the rails frequently, then it's a good time to pause and really think about what you want to accomplish with this book. Sure, you've already assigned yourself a topic and perspective, and you probably have a good draft of an outline already. But what you've told yourself and what you really want are often two different things. And when you're writing a book because you want to write a book, you don't have to suffer. Unless you are on a deadline and money has exchanged hands, you don't *have* to write about anything. Even then, you might have a chance to present your new view in such a way that the client/editor/agent agrees with you!

You may have also noticed that I don't decry rabbit holes completely. I think a good wandering exploration can be handy in nonfiction pieces in order to keep them from becoming too straightforward. Understanding what life was like in Dearborn, Michigan when the first Ford Mustang rolled off the assembly line may not be super important to the evolution of the vehicle itself, but it can provide the reader with a valuable setting where they can rest while you explain the differences in manufacturing between the Dearborn plant of 1964 and the Flat Rock Assembly Plant, where the 2023 Ford Mustang was assembled.

As you practice writing, you'll become more accustomed to recognizing the sensation of falling down a rabbit hole. You'll eventually be able to rein in your research to focus strictly on the points you wish to make, and when writing, you'll eventually discover how to put the pieces together so that your heartfelt joy of sharing your knowledge is properly organized in the context of your book. Alternatively, your editors might kindly share this information with you before you get to the publishing stage, and you'll thank them profusely.

You're also probably starting to get a feel for how all of those things we covered at the beginning of this book—topic, perspective, and organization—can impact your overall writing experience. Not only are these things important for your audience, but I find that figuring these things out before I start writing—rather than bellyflopping onto the pages with aplomb—helps me stay calm and type, even when I'm feeling my least creative.

Now that we know what a rabbit hole is and how to recognize them, let's take a look at how adding detail to your book can actually make your book more valuable for the reader.

Recreating Another Place and Time

When you write a travel book, you take your readers to an entirely different place. They may have seen this place in person, or they may never visit. As a writer, your job is to explain this place to them in a way that allows them to picture it in their mind.

This, in itself, is a major challenge. When I write travel pieces, I'm reminded of the short story "Cathedral" by Raymond Carver. In the story, the author is enjoying a television program about cathedrals, and attempting to share this enjoyment with his wife's blind friend. I encourage you to read it in its entirety, but for the purpose of this example, consider how you would describe a place to someone who had never seen it and has no frame of reference for your description.

Sure, many of us can picture "relentless sunshine" or "mountains as far as the eye can see," but there's a difference between mustering up a decent mental picture and accurately capturing the way it feels when your horizon actually changes. Whether it's the multitude of emotions felt before a big voyage or the carnival of spices used on an unfamiliar local dish, you'll want to select just the right scenes to show your reader in order to fully capture the topic of your travel book.

Historical nonfiction adds yet another dimension to this equation: time. The very definition of historical means that the topic is in the past. Your readers therefore not only have to understand the location of your book, but the historical context, as well. This means educating them on not just the physical surroundings, but the cultural, socio-economical, educational, and religious context within the timeframe of your topic.

What you reveal, however, depends on your perspective. A book about Abraham Lincoln, for example, may or may not need to share his humble log cabin beginnings in order to make its point. Knowing what blue-collar workers in Dearborn did for fun may or may not relate to your examination of how horsepower has increased in the Mustang. On the other hand, it might be appropriate in a book about how trends and social cues have influenced the exterior appearance of the Mustang.

Historical and travel pieces tend to be more detail-oriented than other types of nonfiction, simply because there is so much stage to be set in order for the reader to follow along. As a writer, you'll have to decide which of the details are pertinent to your discussion.

At the very root of your decisions will be your topic, perspective, and organization. If your topic is suitably sized—not too narrow and not too nebulous—it will be much easier to determine what doesn't necessarily need a full poetic waxing and what deserves its own chapter. If you have a well-defined perspective, there will be some clear choices for additional discussion. And if you remain organized, you'll get a better intuitive feel for where all these pieces should fall in your book.

That being said, it takes a lot of practice to become proficient at this. If you revisit the "15 Minute Memoir" exercise, you'll likely notice a lot of parts that could probably be clipped or rearranged before you turned this into a book. You may realize that something you mentioned casually deserves a lot more attention, or that something doesn't necessarily belong anywhere. In my example, I'd definitely cut myself off when it came to the description of crayons. Though that was true and a part of the memory, it doesn't really have to do with the first day of kindergarten, my social awkwardness, or meeting Mindy.

As with rabbit holes, it's a "dealer's choice" situation as to where you direct the readers' attention with your writing. If you really want them to know about the bathrobe you used at the second AirBnB you stayed at, then go ahead and give that robe all of the attention it deserves. But as you're doing so, think of the reader, at home, wondering if that bathrobe is still there... heck, is the AirBnB still open?

As a new writer, I encourage you to just write. You can always remove things in editing, and tidy them up, so they relate more to the story. If you can recognize when your written recreation is becoming an actual rabbit hole and changing the course of your book, then you can avoid a lot of heartaches... but this skill is not always intuitive. You have to do what you think sounds best, you have to get lost a little bit, and you have to forge your own path back to reality, just like Alice. If you don't look at the past hundred words or so and ask yourself, "Wait! What am I doing?" at least a few times, then I envy you.

You are going to go down a few unnecessary rabbit holes, and you are going to find yourself adding unnecessary levels of detail like those decorative throw pillows that people have been obsessed with since the 1990s. You're going to look at your word count and realize that you just fired off 1500 words about late Victorian haberdashery when you were just trying to describe the hat that a British landlord's wife was wearing during the potato blight in order to highlight the role of classism in mass Irish emigration. Don't admonish yourself too harshly when this happens—instead, chalk it up to being part of the process, and if you like what you've written, save it somewhere before you delete it from this draft.

Author's Note: Do You Really, Really, Really Want to Write Non-fiction?

When it comes to recreating another place and time, we may be tempted to fill in the details we don't know with some ideas that we've invented. After all, how many readers can—or will—bother to verify these facts? (Answer: all of them.)

There is nothing more frustrating than having a blank spot on your canvas. As history writers, we often curse our ancestors for not keeping immaculate notes for us about absolutely everything. Presumably, the advent of social media will prevent future generations from ever wondering what we had for dinner, or what the view from the mezzanine looked like the night a show premiered on Broadway. But as for what we're writing now, we may still be waiting for archaeologists to discover the information that would fill in that blank space.

As a travel writer, it may be tempting to invent journeys that simply haven't happened. You can lie on a calm beach somewhere, watching paddleboarders skim across the sunset, and imagine the type of experience they're having. But the second you start to write about it like it's happening to you, you're no longer writing your own account. There may be a very valid reason why you aren't paddleboarding at that exact moment, but you can't accurately present that activity as your adventure.

There are ways around this. First, you can directly tell the audience that this is a blank spot and that you're filling it in with details based on your knowledge:

"While the details of the meetings have been lost to time, we know that Lee Iaccoca's presentation must have been aggressive and exemplary, as the Mustang soon became Ford's top priority. Some speculate that he began with... ."

"As I reclined on the beach, I couldn't help but imagine seeing the world through the eyes of the intrepid paddleboarders who passed silently between me and the setting sun. I could practically feel the... ."

It's acceptable to admit that you don't know something. It's ok to share someone else's speculations with your audience, as long as you properly credit them.

It's also ok to write historical fiction. As we mentioned earlier, these are largely fictional tales based on actual historical events. It is entirely possible that your topic and perspective are best served at a fictional afternoon tea in which George Washington was in attendance, for example. Using what we know and painting a somewhat fictional world around it can be both informative and entertaining for audiences of all ages. You might be familiar with the novel *Gone with the Wind*. The events of the Civil War and Restoration Era described by Margaret Mitchell really happened, but Scarlett and Rhett weren't key players.

You may also want to consider writing a period piece. In this type of fiction, most of the elements are fictional but take place in a specific time and place. *The Great Gatsby* is an example of a period piece, in that it is a social message specific to The Roaring '20s, but the people, places, and events are all fictional. There is a fine line between historical fiction and period pieces, but that more or less comes down to how your book is marketed. As long as you're not trying to pass fiction off as nonfiction, you're doing everything correctly.

Travel-based fiction is also a thing! I truly appreciate this definition of "Travel Narrative," as provided by Benjamin Colbert in The Encyclopedia of Romantic Literature, 2012:

Travel writing is widely considered a hybrid genre, fusing factual reportage with fictional technique, on-the-spot observation with recollections in tranquility, scientific detail with poetic allusion, and verbal description with a visual illustration.

One of the more famous pieces in this genre would arguably be Jack Kerouac's "On the Road." Based on an actual road trip, this novel explores the meaning of life, and whether freedom is possible. Considered one of the significant creations from the Beat Generation, it's a story, social commentary, and a travelogue, all packed together.

Choosing to add the element of fiction to your historical or travel book can be a fantastic, complex opportunity. You'll not only research the facts, but you'll also get to invent your own elements as well!

At the risk of relentless self-promotion, I do encourage readers who are interested in fiction writing to check out my earlier books, especially *One Word at a Time*, which specifically focuses on the fiction-writing process. If at any time it feels like I'm going too fast, it's likely because I'm trying to not be too repetitive.

Now that we've looked at how to recognize rabbit holes, being true to all dimensions of the setting, and determining how much reality is going to direct your writing, it's time to put it all together and take your reader to your topic.

Taking Them There

Picture this: You're at home, curled up in bed. You're wearing your favorite comfy clothes, and you've got a beverage sitting beside you that's exactly perfect for the occasion. You're reading a book, and despite the fact that you are physically holed up in a Minnesota snow squall, the book you're reading about Hawaii has you feeling warm and carefree.

If you've ever had a chance to really dwell on the concept, you may recognize that the human imagination is a very strange thing. Our brains have this function that allows us to take written descriptions and turn them into nearly tangible experiences. With just the right words, we can smell the food cooking in the marketplace, hear the cacophony of voices on the lawn just before the President begins to speak and feel the gentle grit of sand on the soles of our feet.

But I just told you to be wary of rabbit holes, and we've discussed fine-tuning details to those that are factual and necessary. So how are you supposed to take your reader with you through space and time?

Taking your reader where they need to be in order to really experience the topic from your perspective is the top challenge for all writers. There is a sweet spot between brevity and verbosity. There are such things as "too much" and "too little," but your ability to paint a picture for your reader is limited only by what you're willing to put on the canvas.

And like painters, writers have different styles. Despite being contemporaries, Ernest Hemingway and F. Scott Fitzgerald would likely describe the very same glass of absinthe in very different ways. Perhaps the glass, the lighting, the piano playing in the background, or the liquid itself would be the most important, depending on the perspective.

If you are new to the art of writing, you likely don't have an established style yet. This means you'll still find yourself wondering where the "just right" spot is when it comes to detail and description. My advice is to stick with it, keep writing, and read what you've written from time to time to make sure you're sticking to your intended structure.

No one has written the "perfect" book that makes every reader happy, and it's unlikely to happen. What you can do, however, is write the very best book that you can write, right now, given what you've got in terms of experience and knowledge. Your style will develop as time goes by, and you'll get better at seeing when you're about to wander off-topic, and when you're giving the readers exactly the right demonstration of place and time.

When I say "taking them there," I mean allowing your reader to use their imagination to escape their current surroundings and experience the time and place of your book. This can be as simple as adding a few adjectives to a sentence or spending a few extra sentences describing how the scene would be interpreted by the five senses.

Luckily, we have an abundant array of luscious, poignant, pointed, abrupt, bold, flowery, and otherwise descriptive words to help us along our journey. I encourage you to use them at your leisure for your readers' pleasure (and your own).

Let's take a look at a few examples and practice this effect ourselves with this chapter's exercise.

Exercise: The Importance of Show vs. Tell

I am admittedly a huge devotee of show and tell. From the days of holding my favorite stuffed toy high above my head and explaining to my entire kindergarten class how very much Felix the Pumpkin meant to me, to the present day, in which I get to show and tell for a living, I have always adored delivering picturesque descriptions and plain directions.

So, if you're wondering if this is another Lauren Bingham show/tell exercise, I assure you it is. This one is unique, however, in that we're going to focus on a nonfiction topic.

Supplies needed:

- *paper/writing utensil and/or open, blank .doc file, set to your preferences*

- *Your "muse"*

Step 1: Behold Your Muse

I'm calling it a "muse" to be witty, but we're going to need some external support for this one. Find a photo or painting of a place and time that is not here and now. Anything will suffice for this exercise, such as:

- A selfie you took on vacation last year

- A portrait of a famous figure

- A landscape photograph

- A picture of a building you're familiar with

Don't stretch too far or try too hard to find something. The more familiar you are with the picture you choose, the more natural this exercise will feel, but you can do this with a picture of a place or time you've never experienced before.

Step 2: Observe Your Picture

Start jotting down notes about what you see in the photo. They don't have to be coherent or even particularly descriptive. For example, let's say I've chosen a photo I took in 2001 of two of my friends standing in front of the Chicago skyline.

I might start with:

- *It's dark*

- *It's clearly cold outside—people are wearing coats*

- *There's a little bit of snow on the rocks*

- *They're by the lakefront*

- *The city is in the distance, but still recognizable*

Step 3: Tell Me What's in the Picture

Even though the phrase is "show and tell," I find it more helpful to start with the telling, and add the show from there. You may feel differently, in which case, it's perfectly fine to swap this step with Step 4.

Essentially, you're going to tell an imaginary audience about what is in the picture. Whether it's an important dignitary or a little-known spot you visited long, long ago, connect with the picture long enough to tell your reader what's going on.

In my case:

This is a picture of my friends Shaquan and Vickie. It was taken during a trip to Chicago in December 2001. The weather was snowy, and we didn't have much money, so we were taking a walk after dinner and stopped to take this picture with a disposable camera in Uptown with the city lights in the background.

Not bad. A "telling" description is direct, without added color commentary. You've got just enough adjectives to know the who, where, what, when, and how of the scenario. There's nothing wrong with this approach, and there are many cases where "telling" the audience about a scene in a brief and fact-driven manner is appropriate.

Step 4: Show Me What's in the Picture

In this step, we're going to create our own version of the photograph using words. I want you to go all out here. No corner of the picture is off-limits. I want to read about this photograph in words so glorious, so vivid, that I can't help but get a mental picture. In fact, try to get as many senses as possible involved so you can really take anyone reading your description to the scene.

Back to Chicago:

December in Chicago is generally cold, damp, and depressing, though not necessarily in that order. On the night of our visit, we were all feeling a bit grumpy, and the oppressive moist wind that constantly blows by the lake isn't exactly refreshing when your shoes are full of snow.

Still, our spirits were high. We'd just finished off a tasty dinner at the taqueria down the street from our host Shaquan's tiny studio apartment. We'd soaked in the warmth and the most delicious horchata in Uptown before heading out into the darkness. Without too many pennies to our names, our best form of entertainment was walking.

We didn't make it far. The whipping wind, the fullness of our bellies, and the desire to be anywhere that wasn't cold and damp led us to turn around once we got to the lake.

Before we continued our trudge back to the apartment, though, Vickie begged us to take a quick picture of her with the lake and skyline. She asked Shaquan to pose with her, since he had been so kind to host us, and he obliged. Together, they stood with cheeks shiny and pink from the cold, noses dripping, coats disheveled, with the lights of the city glowing radiantly behind them.

Again, this is raw footage, so to speak, so I wouldn't say I followed my own advice here. I didn't mention what they were wearing, what we ordered at the taqueria, our exact path to the lake, and so on.

But, as I've said several times, there's no wrong answer, just as there is no "right" way to do these exercises. What I hope you notice when reading both of your samples is that telling is a much more straightforward type of writing, while showing is more descriptive and often more immersive for your reader.

Here's the tricky part: writing a book that is strictly telling or strictly showing is absolutely exhausting for the author and the reader. Instead, it's best to apply each method in just the right dose. But even worse—there's no golden equation that tells you how much showing and/or telling you should do.

Your personal style will dictate a great deal of how much "flower and spice" you put into your writing. Additionally, some topics lend themselves to detail more readily than others. A 2x4 plank and a 240-year-old tree are not going to provide the same level of fascination or word count.

When I'm trying to decide how much creativity I want to spill onto these pages, I often try to put myself in the position of my reader. Does it make sense to go into deep descriptive detail here? Does it really matter if Shaquan was wearing a green plaid shirt and Vickie was wearing my orange sweater? If I am trying to actually take the reader into that scene, then yes. If I'm trying to be informative of simple facts, then maybe no.

So how do you decide if it's time to take the reader into the scene or whether being informative of simple facts is more appropriate?

Immersing the reader in the scene and putting them in that place and time so completely that they lose track of their current location requires dedication, patience, and impressive powers of observation. If you're the kind of person who gets emotional at the beauty of morning dew on the grass, this type of writing can be pretty intuitive to you.

Informing the reader of facts isn't necessarily as simple as it sounds, either. There's really no such thing as an "event" so much as there are "many things that happened in an increasingly less random way that led up to this event." When writing a history or travel book, it can be very tempting to go into "And Then" mode:

"Then the Beatles decided to go to America. And then they took a plane across the Atlantic Ocean, and then they landed in New York. And then there were a bunch of people waiting for them at the airport."

"Then we went back to the hotel, and then we took a shower and just hung around while we waited for our dinner reservations. And then we took an Uber to the restaurant. It was good. And then we went back to the beach."

"And Then" mode is safe. It's easy. It gets to the point very quickly. But don't you have a few questions when you read those snippets? Don't you want to know just a little bit more?

So how do you go about writing some of the most descriptive nonfiction genres without losing your audience? Patience. Practice. All of the three tenets of "'Good' Nonfiction" as discussed in the first chapter. But mostly practice.

If you intend to publish your pieces, rest assured that your readers will cheerfully tell you exactly what they think of your style. What you do with that information is entirely up to you. I personally like to digest each critique or compliment individually. If I start noticing trends in either column, I'll know that I've got something to work on, or that I've found a sweet spot.

Furthermore, critiques and compliments are just the opinions of one person. Some people like saying nasty things for fun, especially on the internet. Nearly everything I've published has at least one review that was clearly written just to get laughs at my expense. Honestly, I think it might be a lower form of flattery since people have to actually purchase and read my books in order to bloviate about how much they hated it.

Ultimately, you get to decide how you take your readers to the place and time in which your history or travel book takes place. You can go down all the rabbit holes, do all of the research to fill in the blanks, use all the adjectives, and do just as much showing and telling as your heart desires. You can't decide how your readers will react or how much they'll enjoy it, but you do get to choose how much you let that information impact your life and writing style.

Just keep writing, and before long, your style will start to feel more familiar and automatic. Trust me—I write "how-to" books about it!

This brings us to our next nonfiction genre: self-help and how-to books. It's time to tie these two books into our nonfiction fundamentals to create a strong book that provides the intended level of guidance.

SELF-HELP AND HOW-TO

S elf-help and how-to books are often a bit of a delicate area simply because every human is different, and each of us likes to be told what to do in different manners. And, when you write a self-help or how-to book, you are absolutely telling people what you think they should do.

As someone who has penned quite a few "how-tos" and even a couple of self-help workbooks, I will loudly admit that these are some of the hardest to write, emotionally. I know—that is to say, I expect, understand, and fully acknowledge—that someone is going to read my how-to books and say "That's not how you do it at all! How dumb is this writer?"

In fact, there are infinite ways to focus on and better ourselves, just as there is more than one way to skin a knee (to make an old phrase more palatable).

When writing these types of books, you have to be aware that there are people who have found and are extremely comfortable with their own methods. I enjoy having discussions with others in which we share our differing views and processes because you can learn a lot about yourself when you consider other perspectives. Some people are not as open to discourse. These people will still purchase, read, and unilaterally hate your self-help or how-to book at some point.

So, if your motivation for writing one of these books is to be "right" and make everyone realize they've been doing it terribly wrong their entire lives, you will be sincerely disappointed. Forming a cult or changing the world is often more than a one-book effort.

Instead, I like to think of writing guidance books as an option for those who are seeking assistance around a particular topic. I don't claim to be *the* answer, but merely an option. I ask readers to take inspiration from my text, rather than proclaiming it the "only" way.

You have to have a certain amount of confidence to write a guidance book. Some writers are absolutely positive that what they're sharing with their audience is going to revolutionize their way of thinking. Others are hoping to join the conversation on a topic with what they feel is a valid point to make. Most fall somewhere in between.

To put it plainly: readers like to know that their author knows what they're talking about. As they peruse your text, they want to feel assured that you're not just making it up as you go along. Especially in the case of self-help and how-to books, readers want to know that they are following a trusted authority.

In order to do that, you'll want to be a guiding force for your readers. You'll want to come from a place of helping and assistance. Furthermore, you'll want to present your ideas in a way that your reader understands and can follow. And, as you're probably guessing, a lot of that comes down to topic, perspective, and organization.

Let's take a look at the nonfiction principles in action here.

Being the Guiding Hand

For the purpose of this chapter, I'm going to continue under the assumption that you are writing a self-help or how-to book with the intention of others reading it. It's not a requirement, of course, and you're free to hide your book from humanity forever. However, folks don't generally write these types of books if they want to keep the contents a secret. Therefore, the chapters in this chapter will assume deliberate interaction with the reader.

When you're considering writing a self-help or how-to book, there are a few questions you should ask yourself before you get too invested in this project:

- Why do you want to write this book?

- Who are you writing this book for and who do you want to read and follow it?

- Why would someone choose this book over all of the other books on this topic?

- What are you trying to accomplish or what do you hope to be the result of writing this book?

It's ok to be a tiny bit egotistical here. For the most part, the main reason anyone wants to write a guidance book is because they've discovered a method, process, or point of view that is helping them and they wish to share it with others. Approach your book with the understanding that your thoughts are valid, helpful, and worth sharing. Admitting that not everyone will agree with you is an exercise in humility, but once you've become accustomed to this concept, you can write on with the knowledge that your book is worth reading.

That being said, there are things you can do as an author to make the journey as comfortable as possible for your readers.

Once you've identified your motivation behind writing this book, it's time to review your choice of topic and perspective in light of your realizations. Once again, you'll ask yourself the timeless question authors have agonized over since the first written word: "Does this make sense?"

It is highly likely that you'll look at all of the notes and thoughts you've accumulated and feel your throat tighten, your heart starts beating a little faster, and your stomach flip-flops a bit. That's normal. Many people are uncomfortable with stepping into the role of an authority figure, so feeling a little overwhelmed is natural. On top of that, you're likely looking at a whole mess of ideas, and it may not seem like they have any connection to each other. You may be wondering if you just wasted a significant amount of time making an overwhelming mess that you'll have to abandon before it drives you mad.

While you may ultimately decide to start over, this moment of anxiety doesn't necessarily mean you've done it all wrong. Instead, consider this an opportunity to really spend some time with your notes and your topic. You wouldn't have jotted down all of these spur-of-the-moment thoughts if they didn't have some sort of meaning to you.

This may be a great opportunity to start categorizing and organizing your notes. You may have a lot of material on one aspect—a rabbit hole, perhaps—so take the time to put all of the relevant details, links, quotes, and resources together. Come up with a label for each category of notes, such as "Scientific Studies Related to (Topic)," "Historical Facts," or "Step-by-Step Procedures."

This brings me to the next point—writing a guidance book does not exempt you from doing research. Part of filling the role of the "Trusted Authority" means really and truly knowing what you're talking about.

You are the expert on your own self-help or how-to methods, concepts, and processes, but you do need to have some actual facts in there. If you were to write a book on how to change your furnace filter, for example, you would benefit from knowing about the world of filter options, different types of furnaces, why changing a furnace filter is important, the risks of neglecting to do so, and when to contact a professional. You don't necessarily have to cover all of these topics in your book, but being able to confidently and factually explain your recommendations in context will help your reader believe in your credibility.

This is also true for self-help books. If your goal is to help someone change their life, it's a good idea to back your ideas with facts about how making these adjustments can actually benefit them. Sharing the consequences of continuing their behavior can help them appreciate why shifting their perspective might be necessary. Scientific facts, anecdotal evidence, and understanding the theories behind certain behaviors can be helpful as you coax your readers into considering a different process.

I have gone as far as enrolling in courses through community colleges or online learning platforms to make sure I have the right level of confidence to commit to and complete a book. You don't necessarily have to get an advanced degree in your topic, but having a solid background will help you build credibility both as an author and in the text you create.

So, as you're putting everything together, and wondering why you're doing this, and if any of your decisions make sense, consider also how much research you've put into your topic. Doing a little investigation as you ponder your topic can truly help you narrow down your perspective as a guidance book writer, as well. Once again, topic, perspective, and organization weave together to create the net that will guide your book to shore, metaphorically speaking.

Stepping into the role of the "guiding hand" when writing a self-help or how-to book is a little more involved than slapping down a few ideas on paper. You need to connect with the reader as a trusted authority. This may mean taking a good, long look at your motivation, as well as doing any additional research to truly know what you're talking about. Focusing deeply on your topic from a "why and how" angle can help you settle into this role quite nicely.

You'll also want to consider what type of helper you want to be, so let's explore the importance of tone in a self-help or how-to book.

How to Be a Helper

We talked about how your style can impact the overall outcome of your book in the last chapter, but there's a slight difference between your style and your tone. While they do essentially work in tandem, your style refers to the types of words you use, the length of your sentences, the particular adjectives and adverbs you incorporate, and how you weave together your paragraphs. Your tone, on the other hand, directly implies the voice you use when writing your book.

When reading my books, I hope you find the tone lighthearted and friendly. I don't want to come across as a bully. I don't want to pretend I am the only beacon of knowledge in the art of writing. I don't want there to be anything forceful or uncomfortable about my books because in my opinion, writing a book is hard enough without someone barking premonitions of failure towards you.

However, if I were writing about a more dire topic, such as "How to Quit Smoking" or "Overcoming Agoraphobia through Basic Lifestyle Changes," I would likely choose a more serious and straightforward tone. The world will not stop turning if you take five years to write a book. The consequences of tobacco use or facing a major psychological challenge are far more important. (Please note that I say all of this with no judgment towards those who engage in tobacco use or are experiencing major psychological challenges—we all have our things to deal with in our own way!)

Ultimately, the tone of your book is once again your own choice. No one is going to stop you from writing exactly the book you want to write.

That being said, if you are interested in finding a way to be a helper, I encourage you to take the time to explore the tone you intend to use when writing your book.

Your perspective is going to take center stage here. If you're writing from the point of view that the reader desperately needs to follow your advice or bad things will happen, it's more likely that you'll take a direct, no-nonsense tone with lots of wording like "you must," "you will," and "you need to." For example:

If you want to write a nonfiction book, you must put your nose to the grindstone and follow the steps I provide. You will find yourself extremely confused and lost if you don't. You need to understand the consequences of being disorganized and wishy-washy with your topic. I guarantee you'll regret not following my instructions!

Alternately, if you're trying to gently coax someone into the preparation stages of behavior modification, you might take a lighter approach:

Modern science isn't sure why some people feel compelled to write books. But if you find yourself wondering what it would take to write a nonfiction book, then perhaps it's time to consider what the process entails in order to help you decide whether this is something you should try.

So how do you decide? I'm so very glad you asked. Let's look a little deeper at your audience, and what they need from you as the writer of a guidance book.

Author's Note: Connecting with Your Nonfictional Audience with Your Nonfiction Writing

Do you remember way back in Chapter 1, when we thought about who would potentially read our book? Whether or not you went as far as researching demographics, or simply attempted to picture an actual person with your book in their hand, hopefully, you've taken the time to consider who your audience is.

I recommend revisiting the notes you made on this topic from the first exercise and comparing them to your responses to the "Why do you want to write this book" questions from the last chapter.

Look for any discrepancies. If you said you want to write your book to "reform existing bad behavior," but you want your book to be read by young children, you're going to have to really consider how you're going to convince your audience that they're being naughty, but that they can become good children if they just follow your advice.

Likewise, if you're writing a how-to book, consider how much experience your reader has with the topic at hand. Are you writing for absolute beginners, folks who have tried and failed, or those who are near-experts trying to get to the next level?

Knowing who you're writing for will help inform the language and vocabulary you use, as well as your tone. Weaving together your tone with your perspective and style may seem like a daunting task, especially if you're not a well-seasoned author. To be honest, there have been times when I've halted typing in frustration and shouted, "I don't know how to talk to you!" because I found myself sliding into a totally unintended voice.

It is possible to experience difficulty when writing to a particular audience. It may be stressful and uncomfortable to use a tone that isn't your standard way of speaking. You may need to reconsider whether or not you have selected the right audience for you.

Any time you start to get flustered and feel reality spinning away from you, pause. Clear your mind. Take deep breaths or perform mindfulness exercises. There will be days when you'll cheerfully bang out 3,000 words before you finish your morning coffee, and there will be days when you don't get any writing done because you're busy untangling yourself from the knot you've written yourself into. Finding yourself in a predicament doesn't mean you've gone wrong—it just means you need to trace yourself back to where things started to veer off track and figure out the best way to either get back on a course or build a new path.

In order to connect with your audience, you need to not only know what you're talking about, but who you're talking to in the first place. This can be difficult in nonfiction writing because you don't always have sympathetic characters for the reader to love or familiar situations for them to identify with. Instead, you have a bunch of facts that you wish to impart, and in the case of self-help and how-to books, you're trying to actively help them change paths and do things in a specific way.

I encourage you to take your time but don't allow yourself to obsess over whether your tone is exactly right at all times. Your top priority should be getting through the draft. Yes, you should keep yourself in check and stay on topic, keep your perspective even, and remain diligently organized so that you can maintain all of the various "dos and don'ts" that we've addressed so far. But if you turn your brain inside-out trying to make a perfect first draft, you'll quickly become miserable. And while artists of all types are known for suffering for their art, you don't actually have to. It's not a requirement, but if you find yourself experiencing melancholia, insufferable torture, or spending an extraordinary amount of time languishing or lamenting, you're in good literary company. Stay calm; write on.

Edits are always possible. Even something as deeply embedded into every syllable like your tone can be altered and adjusted after you've finished your first draft. It might not be the ideal situation, but neither is melancholia and lamentation. Proceed with your draft with your sanity as a priority.

My advice for those who are attempting to connect with an audience they've never met is to focus on being genuine. Sure, you may need to fine-tune the verbiage in the editing stage, but if you're being authentically passionate about your topic, you will frequently succeed in sounding exactly like the trusted authority your reader is hoping for.

As we're working on some of the finer points of our voice and style, let's drill down a bit into the finer points of organization, as well. Guiding people means keeping them on the right path. And to do that, you'll need to make sure the path is clear and inviting. Let's find out how.

How to How-To

When writing your self-help or how-to book, I highly recommend considering your readers' level of exposure or expertise with the topic and adjusting the format and pacing of your explanation accordingly.

Reflecting on the demographic and perspective you've chosen, carefully consider how much knowledge you're going to need to pack into your chapters. Imagine that when your readers pick up your book, they're being dropped off at the starting point of a brand-new journey. Everyone is going to arrive with their own experiences, challenges, preferences, and opinions.

As the writer, it's your job to figure out what type of guide you're going to be. Where does your readers' journey begin? How are you going to welcome them and get them orientated to your methods and processes? What are you going to do to position them for success?

Again, you'll want to consider how aggressive or gentle you wish to be with your readers. You'll want to consider their skill and comfort level. And while it would be impossible to accommodate every reader, you've already taken the time to carefully select a demographic and perspective and whittled down your topic to best express your thoughts to this chapter of the population. Right?

When writing a self-help or how-to book, you're going to need to first explain to yourself how you're going to lead your reader down this new and exciting path. Consider yourself a tour guide. What steps or features are you going to highlight? How much background information do you want to give your reader to ensure they understand the situation or processes at hand?

What methods do you think will best help them grasp your concepts? I like to include aside "Author's Note" chapters and exercises to engage my readers, along with a Resources chapter to provide you with additional information on topics that I might have skimmed over a bit more than readers wanted. You don't have to use these specific techniques for your own book, but take time to think of any additional steps you can take to help enhance your audience's comprehension and absorption of your book.

You might want to play around with the different steps you provide to your readers. Consider a ramp and a staircase. They both do the same job of allowing folks to travel up or down a change of elevation.

A ramp, however, allows those using it to choose how much space they cover as they move. Stairs, on the other hand, require users to take equally-sized steps in order to complete their journey. As a writer, you can choose between giving your readers a ramp or stairs, depending on the level of detail you provide and how you provide it.

When attempting to take your audience from Point A to Point B, a linear format is often the most direct path. That doesn't mean you won't have a few rabbit holes leading away from the main path, as we discussed, but rather that you'll start at the beginning and finish the book with the knowledge that will change your readers' lives, perspectives, and skill sets. This format often includes several regimented steps that logically build on each other.

The ramp method of guidance is most apparent in the pacing of your book. If you're writing a book about mindfulness exercises for an experienced audience, you don't need to start with the basics of meditation, breathing, and body scanning. You might acknowledge them and build a ramp over them, allowing you to advance quickly to the actual instruction.

How do you do this? Pacing is a great way to keep your readers marching through your piece at the correct tempo. "Pacing" refers to the amount of thought and words you devote to each concept in your book, and how rapidly you transition from idea to idea. On top of that, the words you choose and your sentence structure can establish a rhythm that can break down your thoughts into bite-sized pieces or help your reader cruise up a ramp to the next big consideration. You may notice that my sentences get a bit shorter when I'm trying to make a point that I feel is important. On the other hand, when I want to delight you into remembering and digesting the information I've shared, I'll bloviate a bit with whimsy and self-reflection.

Let's try an exercise to help establish a feel for how how-to. After all, practice is the best way to fine-tune your style and help you appreciate the interplay between all of the painstaking moving pieces that make a successful guidance book!

Exercise: Before We Walk, We Crawl

When we're telling someone how to do something or how to re-consider their current situation, we often use a step-by-step approach to the process. I've done this for all of the exercises in this book so far.

A step-by-step approach takes its name from the basic staircase. You start on the ground floor with no knowledge, then take a step "up" as you gain more knowledge, until at long last, you've reached the next level of mastery. Each step builds upon what you learned in the last one in an obvious, sequential, equally-measured manner.

A linear process to guiding readers to their goals is often simpler for them to follow. Consider your own reading habits to help you appreciate the perspective of your future readers. Most of us have quite a bit going on in our lives, and being able to keep track of which stage of the process we're on will help us stay focused on incorporating your methods into our lives.

In this exercise, we'll approach a process in a step-by-step manner. We'll assume that the reader has so little understanding of the topic that they only picked up your book in order to figure out whether the title was in a make-believe language.

Supplies needed:

- *paper/writing utensil and/or open, blank .doc file, set to your preferences*

- *15 minutes of uninterrupted time, with or without a timer*

Step 1: Choose Your Process

You can decide to write about any activity you want, but here are a few sample topics to help you get started with the brainstorming process:

- How to ride a bike

- How to whistle

- How to wash a car

- How to make the perfect cup of tea/peanut butter and jelly sandwich/casserole

- How to change the toilet paper roll when it's empty surely I'm not the only person who possesses this amazing skill

Make sure that the activity has enough steps to warrant 15 minutes of writing. Otherwise, you'll be desperately filling in the time with nonsense and fluff. Likewise, don't choose a topic that requires several volumes of detailed explanation. This is just a 15-minute writing exercise.

Step 2: Outline Your Steps

Take a few moments to consider the steps involved in the process you're about to explain. Think of the very first thing a person must do in order to take this journey. What preparation is necessary? Then skip forward to what the reader should be able to accomplish when they're done with your instructions. What does success look like?

Now your job is to fill in the steps between "Start" and "Finish." Make some notes to sketch out some of the steps you'll highlight in your exercise.

Step 3: Set the Timer and Start Writing!

Once you're relatively comfortable with the outline you've created, it's time to start writing. Here's what I came up with on the topic of "How to Turn on My Computer:"

While technology has come to unite humanity, it turns out that our tech devices are as different as two humans can be, despite having no sentient attachments.

Most folks turn on their computers by pressing a button or two. I press a button or twelve, depending on what I'm doing wrong on any given day.

I've been assured that the correct method is to first assure that both the monitor and the laptop are plugged into the power strip. In order to streamline this process, I've looped red tape around the monitor cord and green around the laptop's cord. I can easily tell if they're plugged in.

The next step is to make sure the cats haven't unplugged any of the cords that tether the monitor, the laptop, and the router to each other like digital castaways. This is slightly more difficult because I ran out of color-coded tape. However, the cords are so tangled, a light jiggle of any cable will make all of them wiggle, but only if they're plugged in correctly.

Now it's time to start pressing buttons. I like to start with the monitor button, though it really doesn't matter where you start. You'll be pushing everything a few times.

The first time you push the monitor button, it will pop to life in a blaze of white and purple streaks. This is a farce. Turn it off and roll your eyes. Don't believe the lies. After you've counted to 10, press the monitor power button yet again. Nothing will happen. Count to 10 again, and it will splash to life as if nothing has happened with the warning "No Device Detected."

Again, we know this to be false, since we jiggled and wiggled the cords. It's time to engage the laptop itself.

Open the laptop. If the screen remains blank for more than 30 seconds, close the laptop again. Open it again. It should sputter and flash and eventually cough up your screen. Close the laptop. Take a few moments to make sure you're comfortable, have a glass of water, put your phone on the charger, or go to the bathroom. When you return, you should finally have my laptop in full, upright, functioning order.

Step 4: Read What You've Written to See What You've Missed

Since this was a timed writing exercise, it is fairly likely that you didn't include some pertinent details in your step-by-step process. Looking at my own writing, I see I've neglected to mention that the laptop is calmly awaiting your attention on top of my desk. I told the reader to open and close it, but I didn't tell them where to find it or what it looks like.

When you reread your how-to steps, take into account how much detail you've used in each step of the process. Can someone who is reading these directions for the first time visualize or identify all of the moving parts? Are your instructions specific enough for them to follow along?

If you tell someone to, "take a deep breath," for example, are you asking them to take a single deep breath, or do you actually want them to take as many deep breaths as it takes to clear their mind? What type of deep breathing technique do you want them to use? Slow counting inhale? Forceful exhale? Through the mouth or the nose?

Some details can be glossed over–for example, when I explain you'll need a piece of paper or a blank computer document, I'm going to assume that you know what paper looks like and/or how to use your devices. Don't patronize your readers, but recognize that everyone has a different starting point. Everyone has a different understanding of their world, and some folks have more questions than others.

If you leave your reader with too many questions, you'll likely lose their interest after a while. If you have too many gaps in your instructions, your audience will simply stop trying to follow after the first time they get lost.

I encourage you to have someone else read your exercise, too. Ask if they would feel confident following these steps, and what types of questions they have about the process. Ask them if the format is clear, and whether you need to slow down or speed up your steps. Are these appropriate, even baby steps, or are you asking them to tiptoe to the base of the hill, then run up it as fast as they can?

Most folks are hesitant to try new things. The prospect of failure is terrifying. In most cases, it's much easier for all of us to just not do the new thing instead of trying and flailing around with wild incompetence as we try to learn. But as self-help and how-to writers, it is quite literally our duty to encourage people to try and to set them up not necessarily for ultimate success, but at least with the confidence that they can get through the book without feeling attacked, frustrated, or confused. Suffice it to say that readers who feel attacked, frustrated, or confused do not leave happy reviews, nor do they continue to purchase your books.

Writing guidance books such as self-help and how-to pieces can be a bit nerve-wracking. As the writer, you are accepting responsibility for taking your reader on a potentially life-changing voyage. But to do that, you must be a sympathetic and trustworthy guide. How you approach your audience, the tone you use, and the manner in which you take your audience through the process can help them believe not only in you but in the book you've written.

PHILOSOPHY AND INSIGHT/ANALYSIS

W e're going to spend less time discussing the last two nonfiction genres. This is not because they are any less important,
complicated, or deserving of discourse but because we're taking this
chapter as an opportunity to pull together everything we've learned
so far.

In each chapter so far, we've looked at different types of nonfiction
and examined the three major concepts that form the roots of "good"
nonfiction:

- Choosing a topic that isn't too narrow or broad

- Finding a perspective that is unique, informative, and entertaining

- Organizing not only the book itself but your research

From there, we've wandered through a metaphorical garden of
nonfiction touchpoints and techniques:

- Accuracy and your mission as a fact-finder

- Avoiding possible legal woes

- Achieving the right level of detail for your audience

- The importance of background information, related threads, and other "rabbit holes"

- Options for those who wish to explore the line between fiction and nonfiction

- The choice between taming and igniting your descriptive text

- Refining your formatting, tone, and pacing to provide your audience with the most relatable content

We've woven all of these pieces together into a complicated fabric that may more resemble a cobweb than a tapestry at this point. Once again, I urge you to be brave and charge on, confident that one way or another, you'll end up with a first draft of some sort.

Our last two nonfiction genres to cover are philosophy and insight books. These two book types have somewhat of a nebulous definition when it comes to the material covered and how it's structured. In fact, there are some resources that consider these subcategories of self-help books.

Ultimately, these books are written to reveal your individual perspective on a certain topic. If you are offering this perspective with the intention of adjusting the reader's understanding of existence, you are likely writing a philosophy book. If you're writing for the sheer purpose of making your readers aware of your thoughts, opinions, understanding, and conclusions derived from your studies on a topic, this would be considered an insight or analysis book.

Like every type of nonfiction, we've discussed so far, these types of books benefit from the three main concepts and the resulting touchpoints. However, there are a few extra tips that are particularly important for those who are writing philosophy or analysis books.

Specifically, I'd like to devote a couple of chapters to what it means to write a book that comes entirely from your own head... yet is 100% factual.

Uploading Brain-Share Material

Philosophical and insight books are unique—while you still need to have well-researched facts as the basis for your discussion, the rest of the material is based on your own insight and expertise.

This does not mean you get to skip the research step. In fact, you'll likely want to make sure you're well-informed about your topic before you get started. While you may feel confident waxing on about your favorite analysis of a certain situation, you should also actively avoid creating a stream-of-consciousness disaster. Your best tools here are focus, clarity, and knowing the point you're trying to prove.

Each of these tools links directly back to our three concepts of topic, perspective, and organization.

Reflect back to our discussion about rabbit holes and detail. While we addressed those topics in the context of history and travel books, I hope you can also see how running off on every possible tangent might unintentionally confuse the reader of a philosophical or analytical text.

"Focus" means keeping the readers' attention on one idea at a time, and giving them the details necessary to process each step and climb each ramp in a way that makes sense. Focus is a direct descendant of organization and perspective. If your notes and outline are organized in such a way that each of your talking points flows into the next, then you won't have to jar your readers with nonsequiturs, asides, and detours to help them understand what you're talking about.

"Clarity" is a sense of maintaining the same style, level of detail, measurement in steps, and language throughout your text to ensure the reader is able to follow your train of thought. That means putting aside what you understand and how you understand it and making sure that you're communicating your knowledge in a way that others can follow.

When I work on books, I generally go into a state of semi-seclusion so I can focus on the topic and the perspective I've chosen. If I start talking to too many people, I start incorporating their voices and views into my writing, so it's best to stay on the path until I'm done. After a while, I start getting a little desperate to talk to other people, so I ask my friends and family if they'd like to read an excerpt of my book. I do this for two reasons—first because I want to be able to talk about my book with someone in order to feel my way through some of the sticky parts, but also because I want to make sure I haven't created a messy stream-of-consciousness rant. There comes a point where writing a book can kind of feel like talking to yourself through a computer screen, especially if your goal is to share your point of view with others.

Whether you choose to share snippets of your book with others or enlist the help of a paid beta reader or editor, it's helpful to have another pair of eyes scan through the text to help you uncover whether your focus has been as tight as you've expected, and where the clarity stumbles off the path into the obscure.

Then comes "knowing the point you're trying to prove." This may seem a little obvious at first, but if you've ever heard an extremely drunk person try to communicate a simple recollection, you can appreciate how sometimes we think we're staying on topic, but alas, our passion and excitement have caused us to take a leave of logic, and we are far, far off-topic.

When I was in eighth grade, my English teacher spent a significant amount of time teaching us how to write thesis papers. In these papers, we came up with a single statement that we wished to prove throughout our writing, and then each following section provided a fact that we argued as proof of our thesis statement.

Each day we wrote some sort of thesis statement. The minimum length was generally five paragraphs, but the topics covered grammatical rules, the books we were reading, a random poem that had been printed on the chalkboard, or even a short film watched at the start of class.

Writing a philosophy, insight, or analytical book is not unlike constructing a very long thesis paper. While an exploration of certain tangents or rabbit holes may be warranted as part of the journey, you want to be sure that each paragraph supports your thesis statement. Everything you write should be placed on the page with the intention to prove that your point is valid and that delving into this topic with a trusted authority like yourself is a worthy investment of your readers' time.

So, if you take a little extra time in the topic development stage, or revisit your organization stage every time you sit down to write, rest assured that this is time well spent in order to help your audience explore your understanding of this topic with you.

Making People Care

I debated over the title of this chapter for a while because I feel it comes across as too blunt. I couldn't think of another way to say it though. When you're writing a philosophical or insight piece, you need to consider how you're going to find and fascinate your audience.

The reader and the writer have an unusual relationship. The writer has control of the book—the entire experience is in their hands when it comes to what's in the book. The reader has absolutely no say in the matter, and they are at the mercy of the writer when receiving the content for which they have paid.

However, writers, this does not mean you have an unwavering captive audience! Have you ever been to a party or event, and someone starts speaking to you... but never stops? They blather on relentlessly, showing no sign of fatigue as you grow increasingly restless.

When we fear we're being held hostage in person, we often find a polite—if not weak—reason to excuse ourselves from the situation before we reach our breaking point. When readers feel even slightly confused or bored, they close the book, set it down somewhere, and forget about it until they find it again during a thorough house cleaning.

Depending on your literary ambitions, this scenario may not trouble you, and that's fine. What I'm trying to establish is that you have just a small window in which to keep your readers' attention. There are countless books to read and infinite other things a person could spend their time doing—why should they spend precious time reading your book if it's not benefiting them in some way?

Folks can debate endlessly about how much an author "owes" a reader in terms of creating an ideal reading experience. Some say that you lose your integrity as a writer if you pen your books with the intent of curating and maintaining a loyal following. Others believe being authentic to your vision is meaningless if no one is reading your work.

I encourage everyone to develop their own appreciation and understanding of the roles of the reader and writer, especially as you explore both roles yourself. My personal goal is to find a sweet spot where you, the reader, will be both entertained and inspired by my books, even if you don't necessarily learn anything new. I'm here to promote confidence and try new things, not write a best-seller or start a cult. That being said, if you have read and enjoyed my entire catalog, I appreciate you, and thank you for joining me on this journey!

"Making people care" isn't a sworn duty, personal responsibility, or even a technical aspect that can be taught in writing classes. It manifests through an interesting perspective, maintains through impeccable organization, maneuvers the reader along a winding path with detail and format, and mesmerizes them with tone and clarity.

In my opinion, the best way to learn how to write a nonfiction book is to try it yourself. You can start small by doing exercises over and over again. You can write a little bit each day, pows. Or, you can do what I did and accidentally fall into a job of rewriting a 30,000-word piece you were editing as your first major book-writing job and frantically flail about for the next 20 days, pulling in every possible resource to prevent you from failing. I don't recommend it, but it does help with perhaps increasing the amount of time you chain yourself to the desk (metaphorically, of course) as your capacity and curiosity gr motivational issues you might have!

I've been doing this for over 20 years, and I'm thrilled to say that even at this stage of the game, writing nonfiction pieces of any length gets "easier" each time. Though I'm not entirely sure that "easier" is exactly the right word. There are still moments when I curse my own literacy and wonder why I think I ought to get paid for doing this since I clearly have no idea what I'm doing. Generally speaking, a few (hundred) deep breaths later, I can scroll back to where I last remember things making sense, and use my understanding of all of the concepts, elements, and ideas of nonfiction to help me find my way back on path. I've tried different things, practiced various notions, and researched not only what I'm doing by how I'm doing it. As a result, I find it less frustrating and heartbreaking when I have to edit and rewrite myself back to cohesiveness.

At first, trying to do all of the things you've just read about at once will seem impossible. But as you practice, as you write, and most importantly, as you read your own work, you'll start to understand your own patterns. Even better—you'll learn to embrace them, enhance them, and make them your own unmistakable style.

CONCLUSION

"No, I don't want to read your book about how to write nonfiction. I could never write nonfiction. I'd just look at the page and write a sentence and be like, 'Yeah, I'm done.'"

The same friend from the Introduction and I were talking about this very book as I was finishing my first draft.

"What do you mean?" I asked coyly. "Nonfiction means it happened. You just have to write down what was done and said, right?"

He stared at me with the look of someone who had suddenly put two and two together to reach an amazing conclusion. Was nonfiction hard, or was it easy? What if it was somewhere in the mystical undefined world between "simple" and "difficult?"

I looked at him, bemused. "Chocolate?" I asked as I offered him a chunk of my candy bar. Silently, he shoved it in his mouth. "Better thee than me," he replied with a sigh.

I like to help people out. I like to share information, but I like to do so in a way that's meaningful for the person on the receiving end of that information. I have absolutely been that person who holds one-sided conversations at parties (usually unintentionally), and I recognize that I have a lot of passion that needs to be carefully directed in order to be useful to anyone.

Having this mindset and personality is ideal for writing nonfiction books, though certainly, it is not a prerequisite. I would personally state that the only "requirement" for writing a nonfiction book is the desire to write a nonfiction book. Obviously, my friend has no desire to do so, so I wouldn't encourage him to try it. Life is too short to make yourself miserable!

However, if you have gotten through this book, and you're still interested in trying your hand at writing a nonfiction book of your own, please do. Start right now, tomorrow, or next week—whatever timeframe is logical for you. Think about your book. Think about where you want to take your readers (real or imagined), and what you want to cover. How will you bring glory to your topic? What revelations will you make? How many lives will change thanks to you placing your fingers on keys or paper and recording your own words?

That might seem to be an overly romanticized look at nonfiction, but really, it's quite true. Biographies, autobiographies, memoirs, historical pieces, travel books, self-help, how-to, philosophical, and analytical books have the power to inform, entertain, inspire, and encourage people to think or live differently than they are today. We read because we want to understand more perspectives and have adventures beyond our own. Almost everything we read has some sort of impact on us, whether by imparting knowledge, engaging our emotions, or moving us to make changes.

If you flip back to Chapter 1, you'll see some examples of the first notes and outlines I made for this book. You can compare this to the actual final table of contents, as well as your overall draft to demonstrate how things change and evolve in the process of writing a book.

I could have instructed you to follow a step–by–step process because it works perfectly for me, but that's not the how-to book I wanted to write. This is primarily because I don't follow a step-by-step process, and nothing works perfectly for me, ever. That being said, I don't feel qualified to tell everyone how to do something exactly. Instead, I want to guide you through how to start thinking about it. How to engage your brain to consider the important ideas involved, rather than forcing you through processes that might not work for your way of learning, understanding, and doing.

We have covered so much material, and we've looked at many different concepts from different angles. It may be hard to put all of these concepts together until you have the chance to try them out yourself. I've always said that writing is like staring at the world with kaleidoscope attachments on a pair of binoculars, and after reading this, you might understand that metaphor a little more!

I hope that you are inspired to work on your own nonfiction book. I hope you complete the exercises and continue to practice. Whether you are boldly passionate about your work or begrudgingly accepting that writing is something that ultimately gives you great joy despite its many frustrations, I hope you always strive to learn and grow in your own writing.

Now write on!

RESOURCES

As with my other books, I've included a handful of resources. Per reader request, I've categorized them by their relevancy to each section. So, all of the resources for Chapter 2 are grouped together, Chapter 3 together, etc. Fear not—I've labeled them so you aren't blindly clicking on links looking for something vaguely helpful!

Once again, I need to mention that I have no affiliation with any of these resources—I've chosen them strictly based on the fact that I feel they might be helpful for those who are interested in more information on the various concepts I've mentioned in this book.

I also encourage you to use these resources as the entrance to your own research rabbit hole. As writers, we are constantly learning and growing, and sometimes hearing the perspectives of those who have walked in similar shoes, so to speak, can be endlessly helpful—or at least sympathetic!

Enjoy!

General Resources

These are resources that can be helpful for anyone who is brand new to the nonfiction scene.

"How to Write a Book (with Tactics from Best Sellers)"

https://blog.reedsy.com/how-to-write-a-book/

"How to Write a Nonfiction Book: A Step-by-Step Guide for Authors"

https://www.ingramspark.com/blog/how-to-write-a-nonfiction-book-guide-for-authors

"The New Outliers: How Creative Nonfiction Became a Legitimate, Serious Genre"

https://lithub.com/the-new-outliers-how-creative-nonfiction-became-a-legitimate-serious-genre/

SEO Tools - For those who are interested in doing keyword analysis or demographic searches, these pages dive into various tool options and how they work.

Ahrefs: https://ahrefs.com/blog/free-seo-tools/

Semrush: https://www.semrush.com/blog/free-seo-tools/

Forbes Advisor: https://www.forbes.com/advisor/business/software/best-seo-software/

Chapter 2

For this section, I wanted to share a few different perspectives from writers and publishing companies on what it takes to write biographies, autobiographies, and memoirs. I encourage everyone to check out writing blogs such as these not as a way to compare yourself to others, but to gain a feel for how all writers deal with challenges differently, and take inspiration and hope from what they share.

"Autobiography vs. Biography vs. Memoir"

https://www.blurb.com/blog/memoirs-biographies-autobiographies/

"How To Write An Autobiography, A Biography and Memoir."

https://www.creativewritingnews.com/how-to-write-an-autobiography-a-biography-and-memoir/

"How to Write a Biography: 8 Steps for a Captivating Story"

https://www.tckpublishing.com/how-to-write-a-biography/

"How to write an autobiography: 7 key steps"

https://www.nownovel.com/blog/how-to-write-autobiography/

"Memoir vs. Autobiography: Which Should You Write?"

https://www.dudleycourtpress.com/memoir-vs-autobiography-which-should-you-write/

Chapter 3

These resources specifically help writers connect history and non-fiction, as well as put their travels into words.

"Six Ways a Historian Can Help You Write a Nonfiction Book"

https://www.thewritersforhire.com/six-ways-a-historian-can-help-you-write-a-nonfiction-book/

"Writing Historical Fiction Vs. Creative Nonfiction | Writer's Relief"

https://writersrelief.com/writing-historical-fiction-vs-creative-nonfiction-writers-relief/

"8 Travel-Writing Tips From Professional Travel Writers"

https://www.grammarly.com/blog/travel-writing-advice/

"Cathedral," by Raymond Carver (as mentioned as an example)

http://www.giuliotortello.it/ebook/cathedral.pdf

Chapter 4

Here you'll find a few interesting selections for those interested in writing self-help and how-to books. You may find that the ideas in these links can apply to each type of book!

"A Guide to Writing Self-Help"

https://nybookeditors.com/2017/06/guide-writing-self-help/

"The 3 Golden Rules Of Writing A Self-help Book"

https://www.standoutbooks.com/how-to-write-a-self-help-book/

"How to Write a "How To" Book By Susan Bilheimer"

https://writersweekly.com/this-weeks-article/how-to-write-a-how
-to-book-by-susan-bilheimer

Chapter 5

And lastly, look at philosophical and insight/analysis pieces. You'll find these links come from academic resources. Given that philosophical and insight pieces have a background in educational environments, it stands to reason that some of the strongest guiding hands in these areas are actual educators. Don't let words like "paper" or "literary" throw you off—I felt the concepts in these resources were strong enough to benefit book writers such as yourself!

"A Brief Guide to Writing the Philosophy Paper"

https://philosophy.fas.harvard.edu/files/phildept/files/brief_guid
e_to_writing_philosophy_paper.pdf

"A Short Guide to Close Reading for Literary Analysis"

https://writing.wisc.edu/handbook/assignments/closereading/

REVIEW

Reviews and feedback help improve this book and the author. If you enjoy this book, we would greatly appreciate it if you could take a few moments to share your opinion and post a review on Amazon. Thank you!

Also By Lauren Bingham

How to Write a Book: A Book for Anyone Who Has Never Written a Book

One Word at a Time: How to Write a Fiction Book for Beginners

Just Write: A Calming, Realistic, and Optimistic Approach to Writing Your First Book

www.ingramcontent.com/pod-product-compliance
Lightning Source LLC
Chambersburg PA
CBHW071204120626
46546CB00006B/2402